Coming Home To Yourself

Coming Home To Yourself

A Soulful Guide for Women in Midlife

Ann CB Landis

Copyright © 2025 by Ann CB Landis
All rights reserved. No part of this book may be reproduced, stored in a retrieval system, or transmitted in any form or by any means—electronic, mechanical, photocopying, recording, or otherwise—without the prior written permission of the copyright owner, except for brief quotations used in reviews or critical articles.

ISBN:
978-1-946240-06-4 (paperback)
978-1-946240-07-1 (ebook)

Printed in the United States of America

First Edition

For more information, visit:
annlandis.com

for all our mothers

Introduction

The Threshold

The first half of life is about becoming who you needed to be to survive. The second half is about unraveling everything that no longer aligns with your soul's purpose. That's not a midlife crisis—it's a rebirth.

Ella Hicks

When I was 13, I decided I would never turn into my parents.

It was 1988, and my mom and dad both worked in the schools. Mom taught middle school home economics or, as she described it, "cooking, sewing and sex." She was always bringing colorful stories to the dinner table.

One was about a boy who recoiled at an illustration of the male reproductive system, which Mom had slapped onto the overhead projector. She was about to use her pen to point to all the parts as she explained their function. The boy exclaimed, "Mrs. Bevans, don't *touch* it!" My mother managed to keep her composure long enough to run into the hallway, where she doubled over in laughter, out of earshot of her students. As a middle school sex ed teacher, Mom ran into the hallway a lot.

Dad was an assistant principal at a different middle school. During the year, his job was to discipline kids who broke the rules, including chastising their parents as appropriate. In the summer, he stood with his tall frame bent over the kitchen table, fiddling with a board that had pins sticking out of it. They were arranged in a grid, with the columns representing days and the rows representing periods. Then he used a gajillion little tags to organize the class schedule for the following year.

It turned out the job was perfect for him. To say he expected a lot of his students (and my sister and me) would have been a gross understatement. And he was a savant at organizing all the classes offered at his school into five seven-period days so that every teacher had the right number of students, preparations, and planning periods, and every child had the right schedule for their grade and level of achievement. He saw it as his special challenge, and he was insufferable the entire time. Anything that broke his concentration, such as the refrigerator opening or a hand in the cookie jar, was a capital offense.

My parents married four months into a whirlwind romance in 1974. My mother was a force of nature. I don't think Dad knew what hit him. But he was smart enough (at the ripe old age of 39) to put a ring on it. I was born 11 months later, then my sister Katherine came along two years after that.

By the time I was 13, our family had settled into a predictable, mind-numbing rhythm. Dad's alarm went off at 6:30. He sat on the edge of the bed longer than I could fathom trying to wake up, then selected his outfit from a chart he hung on the door, which ensured he didn't wear the same suit and tie combination more than once a month. Mom yanked her girdle on and made breakfast for my sister and me before heading to work in her gray Chevy Celebrity.

As was typical in those days, Katherine and I got ourselves to the bus stop and let ourselves in when we got home from school. Mom and Dad appeared a little later. Mom made dinner. We ate, then asked to be excused. After Dad loaded the dishes into the dishwasher *just so*, we would all pile onto the sofa to watch television until bedtime.

I hated it.

It wasn't so bad when I was small. Maybe TV was just better back then. (Tuesday nights were my favorite, because that's when *The A-Team* was on.) Or maybe I was too young to notice how tired my parents were, probably due to the fact that they ate too much and got zero exercise. (Definitely not throwing stones there.)

The point is, the year I turned 13 I was so over it. At the ages of 53 (Dad) and 42 (Mom), it looked to my youthful eye that they had already given up. They had resigned themselves to an unending, monotonous slog, punctuated by an annual trip to the beach and occasional weekend "naps" behind a locked bedroom door.

I observed this and reasoned that life was like a perilous mountain trail. You spent your childhood running uphill, careening around switchbacks and leaping over rocks and twisted tree roots. Then, at midlife, just when you reached the summit, you immediately ran straight off a cliff. You looked around for two seconds, feet still churning like Wile E. Coyote, before noticing the ground was suddenly a long way down. This, of course, initiated a dizzying tailspin into old age, where life ended in a little poof. It seemed to me that both of my parents were already falling.

Now, I'm about to turn 50. My son is an adult (only just!). Both of my parents have already poofed out of this earthly plane. And I'm realizing that midlife is not a cliff—it's a threshold.

The first half of life demands so much of us. We learn to survive, perform, and prove. We twist ourselves like pretzels into shapes that fit other people's expectations. We chase careers, relationships, children, and approval. We do what it takes to be successful by the world's standards, even when it causes us to forget who we are.

For me, success looked like achievement. It looked like overwork, over-delivery, and saying yes even when my whole body screamed no.

Then, I reached a magical tipping point. I decided I wasn't going to live for other people. I decided to follow my dreams. I got divorced (for the second time), married (for the third time), and along the way spent a few glorious years rediscovering myself.

The threshold is not where you've been, but it's not yet where you're going. It's a liminal space, a doorway between old ways of being and new possibilities. And it's scary, disorienting, and charged with potential.

During this transition, life isn't asking you to push harder. It's asking you to listen. To unravel what no longer fits. To return to what matters.

Don't Call it a Crisis

Our society has a solid definition for a man's midlife crisis. New girlfriend, new car, maybe a new watch or a motorcycle or a speedboat. But what about us?

You already know that our culture doesn't have a framework for the possibilities that open up for women at midlife, apart from telling us that this is the time when our chin hairs turn black and our bellies and boobs start to sag. You're expected to cut your hair short, don a visor, and join the neighborhood power-walking group.

Lies.

Unraveling is sacred work. As your children go off to college and your parents head off into the sunset, your exhaustion and dissatisfaction catch up with you. You sense that your old way of being doesn't match who you are now.

These are not signs of failure, but of readiness.

I believe midlife is the soul's invitation to be reborn. The unraveling feels like the end, but it's really the beginning. The beginning of the story of you.

The good girl, the overachiever, the survivor—they've gotten us this far. But they are not who we are. When they fall away, we are not diminished. We are revealed.

Where We're Headed

This book is not a lecture. It's a companion, a string of lanterns that will light the path from a season of descent, to initiation, and finally to rising.

Part One: Descent

This is the unraveling. The letting go. The painful awareness that the old ways no longer work. You'll meet the Good Girl, who is asleep on her feet. You'll draw yourself a new map that reflects what's left behind after certain things end, and you'll learn to listen to the wisdom of your body.

Part Two: Initiation

Then comes the pause, the tipping point, the quiet place where you remember the girl you once were, claim the stillness you need, and invite magic back into your life. It's not a single moment. It's a period of introspection that asks you to learn to be without doing. During this time, you weigh each aspect of your life so far and decide what to keep and what to release.

Part Three: Rising

Finally, we arrive at rebirth. This is where you get to rewrite the rules and become the woman you were always meant to be. In this stage, you'll design a life that makes room for the people, spaces, and activities you choose.

If that sounds good to you, you're in the right place.

How to Use This Book

This book is designed to be both a reflection and a guide. In each chapter, you'll find:

- Stories drawn from ancient myth and modern life, designed to help you see your own journey in a new light.
- Gentle practices you can try in everyday life, including small steps, simple rituals, and journal prompts to draw out your own wisdom.
- A closing invitation to carry with you as you step back into your everyday world.

You don't need to rush. You don't need to do it all at once. Pull up a chair. Linger. I made us some tea from the herbs in my garden. Savor it as you reflect on what got you here and where you're headed.

Your Journey Begins

If you are drawn to this book, chances are something in your life is shifting. Maybe you feel restless or tired of performing. Maybe your body is screaming at you to just cut it out already. Maybe you've lost something—a job, a role, a relationship—and you're not sure what comes next.

I want you to know there's nothing wrong with you. You are not broken. You are becoming.

Turn the page to join me in the in-between. You don't have to have it all figured out. You only have to be willing to listen and trust.

Together we'll descend, initiate, and rise. Together we'll come home to ourselves.

A Note on Identity and Context

Before we go any further, I want to name the lens I'm writing from. I am a white, straight, cisgender woman who grew up in a middle-class suburban home. That is the body and the life that shaped my perspective. But the truths I write about—the ache for authenticity, the longing to come home to yourself, the quiet courage of choosing a different path—belong to no single identity or background. My hope is that something in these pages reaches you wherever you are, in the fullness of your own ancestry and lived experience, and that you feel welcome to take what resonates and leave what doesn't.

A More on Identity and Context

Part One

Descent

> "Midlife is not a crisis. Midlife is an unraveling. A time when you feel a desperate pull to live the life you want to live, not the one you're supposed to live."
>
> Brené Brown

Part One

Descent

I have loved horses since the day I was born.

I don't remember the first time I saw a picture of a horse or saw one in real life. I can't explain where the obsession came from. But I do remember one time, in first grade, when I was reading aloud with some other children, and I came to a word my teacher was sure I wouldn't know.

Longe line.

A longe line (pronounced "lunge line") is a long rope you attach to a horse's halter when you're working with them from the ground. The length allows them to move around you in a big circle, and you can give them signals to speed up or slow down or change gaits.

If I'd sounded it out, I probably would have said "long line" or "long-ee line." But I said "lunge line," like it was the most obvious thing in the world.

My teacher was flabbergasted.

"How do you know that word?" she demanded.

I shrugged and said, "I just...like horses a lot?"

Remind me to check the Akashic records for a past life explanation, because it's *that weird* that I knew this word.

By then, I was playing with imaginary horses everywhere I went. I saw them running alongside the bus on my way home from school. I drew them on the backs of every homework assignment and all over the grocery bag covers my mother taped onto my textbooks.

Shall I go on? I read *The Black Stallion* by Walter Farley so many times that the library was like, "Aw, just keep it." I measured the size of our suburban back yard to determine if we had enough space for a pony. Spoiler: we didn't.

I begged my parents to let me take riding lessons. I was relentless. Finally, just after I turned eight, they gave in.

Honestly, that was the best day of my life.

But get ready, because here comes the twist.

My parents had absolutely no idea why anyone would want to straddle a horse and ride it around. They hated every part of it. They didn't want to drive me to lessons or pick me up. They didn't want to take me to buy a helmet. They didn't want to pull my big rubber boots off.

They weren't just disinterested. They were steadfastly against anything and everything that had to do with horses.

On the other hand, my dad was a musician.

In addition to his day job telling kids to "clear their area" before they left the cafeteria for fifth period, Dad had been a band leader for 25 years. He was the musical director of countless theater productions, led three choirs, and played organ in church on Sundays.

Dad had lived and breathed music since he could synchronize his fingers. He once told me that, when he was a teenager, he didn't really care about school because all he could think about was being in a big-time band one day.

Basically, Dad loved playing music as much as I loved horses. And as far as he was concerned, I was going to love playing music too.

So we reached a point, when I was about 15, when Dad gave me an ultimatum:

> "You can either keep taking 'cello lessons, or you can keep riding horses. But not both."

I wish I'd said, "I'll stick with horseback riding, Dad, because that's what I really love more than anything."

But I didn't.

I couldn't.

I wasn't *supposed* to.

To this day, playing the 'cello is the main thing people who knew me as a child remember about me.

And it wasn't even mine.

How Unraveling Shows Up

Unraveling doesn't arrive with a neon sign. It slips in quietly.

Maybe you notice it at work. The job you once tolerated now feels unbearable. You can't bring yourself to answer another email, sit through another pointless meeting, or force a smile at another boss who doesn't even know what you do.

Maybe it shows up in your relationships. The distance growing between you and your partner. The ache of leaving children behind when you drop them off at college. The old roles that no longer fit.

Or maybe it shows up in your body. The exhaustion you can't sleep off. The hot flashes, the weight shifts, the restless nights. The body saying no when your mind is still trying to say yes.

My unraveling showed up in a zoom call for a group coaching program I'd signed up for. It was about the 8th chakra. And something about that content and those women and that moment caused me to say, "I'm not a musician."

My classmates kind of blinked at me because they didn't understand the heaviness of those words.

I had come to believe that I WAS a musician, just like my dad. Because I was supposed to be.

But I wasn't.

I was something else all along.

Why We Resist

We are not taught to welcome unraveling. We are taught to fight it, hide it, deny it.

From the time we're girls, we're trained to be good. To keep the peace. To smile even when we're dying inside. To produce, achieve, and maintain. Unraveling is messy, and messiness is not rewarded.

But there's even more to it than that. If you allowed yourself to see how you have compromised, how you have become what you were supposed to be instead of what you really are, it would mean you'd been living someone else's life for a long, long time. And that is just about the most painful realization I can think of.

So, instead of unraveling, we pull ourselves together. We buy the face cream. Join the gym. Hustle harder. Pretend we're fine.

We are not fine.

I tried. I tried to keep the mask on. Tried to push through the exhaustion, silence the doubts and numb the grief. I probably tried twice as hard after I uttered those four little words of truth than I ever had before. For a while.

But masks are heavy, and eventually they start to slip. It may not feel like it at the time, but that's when the fun starts.

The Gift of Unraveling

The thing about unraveling is it's both terrifying and liberating. Terrifying because we're losing what we knew. Liberating because we're finally free to step out of the roles and stories that bound us.

In unraveling, we discover what's left when pretenses fall away. We discover the raw, pulsing truth of who we are.

It doesn't happen overnight, and it doesn't happen neatly. Sometimes unraveling feels like freedom, like pulling your bra through the armhole of your shirt at the end of the day.

Other times it feels like those dreams where you're late for your final exam, only to realize you haven't been to class all semester, and... oh yeah...you're naked.

Whichever kind of day you're having, unraveling is making space. Clearing ground. Softening the soil. Preparing you for new growth.

What's Coming Up

In this section, we'll walk through the descent. We'll name the unraveling, even when it feels uncomfortable. We'll stop pretending to hold it all together and allow ourselves to release what no longer fits.

In Chapter 1, we'll talk about the roles we've carried, the people-pleasing, the overachieving, the endless giving, and how exhausting it all is. We'll explore what it means to set down the mask of the Good Girl and begin to honor the woman underneath.

In Chapter 2, we'll face the emptiness that comes when roles shift or relationships end. That space can feel frightening, but it's also fertile ground. Together we'll learn to see the spaces that are left behind, not as voids, but as clear spaces to choose again.

In Chapter 3, we'll listen to the wisdom of our bodies. The aches, the fatigue, the shifts of menopause—even the black chin hairs—are information. Our bodies are not betraying us. They're calling us home.

Invitation

So here we are, at the beginning of the descent. It may feel like a fall from a high cliff, but it's not. You are not falling apart. You are unraveling into truth.

Have you ever unraveled a sweater all the way? What are you left with? Yarn. *Lots of yarn.* And, more importantly, the possibility of a new sweater.

You don't have to rush. You don't have to know what comes next. All you have to do is pull that first thread.

Chapter 1

The Good Girl is Tired

"Be a good girl."

That was my grandfather's advice on my wedding day. He offered it emphatically, gripping my manicured fingers in his gnarled ones.

I'll admit, I was distracted—there were so many people to greet that day—but he wasn't going to let me go until I looked him in the eye and said, "I will."

To be honest, it seemed superfluous. The exhortation to be a good girl was not new to me, as I'm sure it's not new to you.

From birth, we are steeped in Good Girl culture. Smile. Be polite. Work hard. Don't rock the boat. And my favorite, which my mother offered with rare sincerity: "It's a woman's job to let her husband think he's in charge while she runs everything."

Replace "husband" with any other word. Because how you do one thing is how you do everything.

The Good Girl is a mask that fits so well, we don't even know we're wearing it. But at some point—often right in the thick of midlife—the mask starts to wear and crack. The Good Girl is tired.

This isn't the kind of tired that sleep fixes, though heaven knows you've tried. It's a bone-deep weariness that no nap, no yoga class, no green smoothie can touch.

You've collapsed into bed early, curled up in weighted blankets, put lavender oil on your pillow. Me too. I even put duct tape over the little light on the smoke detector. Nothing worked.

This is the tiredness of being agreeable, responsible, and dependable for so long that you've lost track of who you are. You've packed every lunch, folded every load of laundry, and accepted every work assignment, but you can't pick your own ice cream flavor because you honestly have no idea what you prefer.

If you have a track record of smiling when you'd rather scream, nodding when you want to walk away, or saying "it's fine" when it absolutely *is not*, you are living a life that prioritizes everyone else's comfort at the expense of your own truth.

Are you ready to put it all down? Probably not. Not all at once. But we can start small. Inanna can show us how.

Meet Inanna

In Sumerian mythology, Inanna was the goddess of love, fertility, and war. She was queen of heaven and earth, radiant with beauty and power. Her shining crown, jewels, and fine garments reflected this.

But there was one place where Inanna held no sway—the underworld. There, her sister Ereshkigal ruled, isolated and feared. She was associated with death, grief and silence.

Although they were sisters, they embodied opposite realms: sky and underworld, vitality and decay, desire and inevitability.

One day, Inanna heard a cry from below. Ereshkigal was mourning the death of her husband.

The Good Girl would go to her sister out of empathy or obligation, perhaps to provide comfort, but that was not Inanna's intention.

Some say Inanna decided to travel to the underworld because she was driven by ambition and saw an opportunity to extend her rule. She refused to let any power exist beyond her reach.

Other versions of the myth imply Inanna's descent was an allegory reflecting cycles of fertility and the seasons, similar to the Greek myth of Persephone.

I prefer the version where Inanna's descent was simply inevitable. No one, goddess or mortal, can escape death. In this interpretation, the journey is a metaphor for facing shadow, loss, and the limits of power.

For one of these reasons, or perhaps more than one, Inanna felt compelled to go.

Her friends and servants warned her that facing Ereshkigal would be perilous. They begged her to stay. But she would not be swayed.

Before leaving, Inanna told her trusted servant, Ninshubur, to wait three days. If she had not returned, Ninshubur would go to the temples of the great gods and plead for help. She then donned her finest armor and jewels and set out for the underworld alone.

At the gates, Inanna demanded entry in the name of heaven and earth. Ereshkigal was furious at the intrusion into her realm. No queen would allow another to waltz into her territory unchecked. So Ereshkigal told her servants to allow Inanna's passage, but to require her to remove one of her garments or symbols of power at each of the underworld's seven gates.

At the first gate, Inanna left her crown. At the second, her scepter. Then her necklace, breastplate, golden ring, and breastpin. At last, at the seventh gate, Inanna removed her luxurious robes and entered Ereshkigal's throne room naked and bowed.

What was Inanna's reward for enduring this humiliating and brutal descent?

Ereshkigal struck her dead. On the spot. No drama, no villain soliloquy. She immediately killed her and hung her naked body on a hook, like a piece of meat.

Yeah. Sorry about that. I don't make the myths.

But Ereshkigal didn't gloat. The myth says she fell to the ground, moaning and wailing "as if in childbirth." This reads like sorrow and regret, but I think that's our modern sensibility sneaking in. Perhaps existential pain is just a natural consequence of both birth and death.

Inanna's body remained on that hook for three days.

Meanwhile, Inanna's servant, Ninshubur, kept her promise. She went to Enlil, god of air, then to Nanna, the god of the moon, but both refused to help.

Finally she visited Enki, god of wisdom and waters, who agreed to intervene. Enki fashioned two tiny beings from the dirt under his fingernails and gave them the food of life and the water of life.

These beings, the kurgarra and galatur, slipped into the underworld unnoticed. When they reached the throne room, it was chaos. Ereshkigal was wailing and beating her fists on the floor, and Inanna was—well, you remember where she was.

The kurgarra and galatur assessed the situation and made a plan. Instead of trying to overcome Ereshkigal, they burst into tears, empathizing with her pain. Moved by their compassion, Ereshkigal offered them a favor. They asked for Inanna's corpse. They sprinkled the food and water of life on the body, and Inanna was revived.

Of course, there was a catch. No one could leave the underworld freely, not even a goddess. As Inanna ascended, demons snapped at her heels, demanding a substitute. They continued to follow her all the way back to her palace.

Once there, Inanna met her friends and servants. They were all deep in mourning at her loss, then overjoyed to see her return. Inanna spared them all.

Finally she entered her throne room, and there she found her husband, Dumuzi, sitting on her throne. He was dressed in splendor and was decidedly not grieving.

Inanna immediately fixed the eye of death upon him and the demons dragged him straight to the underworld.

Whew. Quick pause to appreciate the sweet relief of a happy ending.

Like all mythology, this isn't just a story about gods and demons. It's a map of transformation. Inanna shows us how to take off the Good Girl mask and step into our truth.

Zero meat hooks required. Probably.

Inanna's Transformation

In order to understand how this ordeal transformed Inanna, let's take a closer look at the items she surrendered during her descent. But first, what do we mean by "surrender"?

Surrender isn't about weakness or loss—it's an act of transformation. Each time Inanna laid something down, she released a layer of performance—the ways she had learned to prove herself, please others, or control how others saw her.

Performance is the Good Girl's armor. Inside it, she feels protected and safe, but it also keeps her disconnected from her truth. By surrendering these outer roles and masks, Inanna prepared to uncover her true power.

Her Crown

At the first gate, Inanna left her crown. The crown is a symbol of authority, sovereignty and the right to rule. In other words, she surrendered her status.

We all demonstrate our status in different ways. Maybe you're the president of the PTA at your child's school, or you serve on the board of the Homeowners' Association. Maybe you're an entrepreneur or an expert of some kind. Maybe you're a soccer mom, a horse mom, a dance mom. Or maybe you're the one who organizes food trains for ailing coworkers or makes sure no one's birthday gets forgotten or welcomes new people to the neighborhood with your famous chocolate chip cookies.

Here's the key question: in your daily life, how do you prove to others that you're a Good Girl? Surrendering your crown requires you to take a hard look at your methods and decide, are they expressions of your true nature? Or are they just performance? Keep what's real and discard the rest.

Her Scepter

Next, Inanna put down her scepter. The scepter is a symbol of judgment and wisdom. When she left this behind, she surrendered control and the authority to define reality.

Being the Good Girl means following the rules. You know exactly what they are, even if you can't name them. You say yes when you wish you could say no, stay quiet when you long to speak, run yourself ragged to make sure everybody else's needs are met.

Just when you think you know how the game works, midlife comes along and notifies you that you don't know anything. The rules you have lived by, defended, and perhaps taught to your daughters are made up, invented by people and systems that never knew your heart.

The second gate asks you to see that what you thought was real and necessary might be a phantom, the ghost of somebody else's life. Surrendering your scepter means releasing the illusion of certainty and control and making space for a deeper kind of wisdom.

Her Necklace

At the third gate, Inanna left her necklace. The necklace, made of precious stones, represents wealth, beauty, allure and charisma. When she put it down, she surrendered her ability to wield social power and charm.

Listen, I'm not ready to climb aboard the train to Hagsville and neither are you. Putting down your necklace does not mean you're losing your beauty or charisma. Far from it.

It means releasing the compulsion to look and act in ways that please other people. When you lay this down, you also release the pressure to perform a version of yourself that feels acceptable. You stop carrying the weight of other people's expectations about what it means to be you.

Her Breastplate

At the fourth gate, Inanna removed her breastplate. The breastplate represents sexuality, fertility, and seduction—the outward expression of her erotic power. When she laid it down, she surrendered her need to wield magnetism and creative potency as tools of influence.

For much of our lives, we're taught that a woman's power lies in how she's perceived: how she looks, how she moves, how she attracts attention. We learn to use charm or sensuality to feel wanted, to create connection, or to feel safe in a world that rewards beauty and punishes aging, softness, or difference.

But true erotic power isn't something you perform—it's something you embody. When Inanna removes her breastplate, she isn't rejecting sensuality. She's reclaiming it from the gaze of others. She no longer needs to use her allure to feel powerful. She becomes the source of power itself.

Putting down your own breastplate doesn't mean you stop being magnetic. It means your magnetism begins to flow from within rather than being projected outward for approval. It's the moment your creative energy stops working for validation and starts working for you.

Her Golden Ring

As she passed through the fifth gate, Inanna removed her golden ring, a symbol of commitment, connection, pacts and sacred bonds. This act loosened her ties to others, asking her to surrender all the relationships and promises that once defined her.

At midlife, relationships change. Sometimes they end. Sometimes new ones begin. This isn't limited to romance. Think about how your relationship with your child shifts when they move out, or how everything feels different after the loss of a parent.

When my dad died, I remember looking around and thinking, *There's been a mistake. Who left me in charge?*

Like all the gates, this one invites both fear and freedom. Taking a hard look at your agreements—spoken and unspoken—means realizing that your relationships don't simply happen to you. You have the power to choose: who to release, who to keep close, and how to love from a place of truth rather than obligation.

Her Breastpin

The breastpin denotes rank or magical strength. Leaving it behind removed Inanna's ability to act, command, or direct energy. This is a surrender of agency.

At first, that sounds frightening. Agency is how we move in the world, how we make things happen. But sometimes life *does* just happen to us. You can call it chaos, fate, or divine timing. Whatever language you use, this gate is about recognizing that you're not always in control.

Maybe you think it's all random. Maybe you believe you're under the protection of a loving deity. Maybe you're somewhere in between. The truth is, none of us has all the answers. None of us can see life from such a height that we know whether what's happening is good or bad.

This is the gate of surrender to flow. Ask life for clues. Stop pushing, and start listening. Lay it all on the table and see what wants to emerge.

Her Royal Robes

Finally, at the entrance to Ereshkigal's throne room, Inanna removed her luxurious robes, surrendering her dignity, identity, and persona. She was naked—stripped of all protection. This is the surrender of self-image itself.

At this point, there's nothing left to hide behind. No status, no certainty, no charm, no control. Just truth. The descent took everything she used to define herself, leaving only what could not be taken away.

This is the moment many of us meet in midlife—the unraveling of roles, identities, and illusions we've worn for decades. It can feel like death, but it's also the threshold of rebirth. When there's nothing left to prove, you finally become who you've been all along.

At the end of the descent, we are a blank canvas. Only then can we paint ourselves anew, in the colors we choose. You have to let it all go before you can begin again.

Your Descent

I know what you're thinking: How could I possibly let everything go like Inanna did?

I've got good news and bad news.

Good news: You don't have to seek out the descent. If you're meant to go, life will open the gates for you. Descent is a journey—a passage through the initiations that find us when it's time. You will move through them one loss at a time, whether by choice or by circumstance, and each one will bring you a little closer to the truth.

Bad news: You don't get to opt out. If you resist the call, life will keep turning up the volume until you have no choice but to listen.

My own descent didn't begin as a conscious choice. It arrived as crisis—a cancer diagnosis that left me sobbing on the white tile floor of my bathroom, raging at the universe and asking over and over who would raise my two-year-old son.

It deepened as I endured treatment, clinging to the hope that I would have another baby, only for my husband, Dave, to announce that he was finished having kids and would not be swayed.

Shortly after that, my mother fell ill, forcing me to face the shadows of my childhood and ask painful questions about our relationship and why it had been the way it was.

Through all of this, my career took a back seat. The business I had built over many years all but evaporated.

There were so many hits. So many losses. Over and over, life held up a mirror, showing me every place I had been performing—trying to be the best daughter, the best wife, the best entrepreneur—and revealing how hollow those roles had become.

Of course I fell short. Because none of it came from me—from who I really was, or who I came here to be.

This is your Wile E. Coyote moment. Your legs are still churning, but you're not getting anywhere because there's no ground beneath your feet. And you're about to look down.

The alternative to falling is flying. But you can't fly if you're weighed down by everything you've been carrying—the mask you're wearing, the expectations you're still meeting, and the commitments you can no longer bear to keep.

When I first learned Inanna's story, I was confused by Ereshkigal's lament. It seemed strange that someone so cold would weep.

But here's the thing: Inanna and Ereshkigal are two sides of the same coin. You are both Inanna, called to enter the darkness, and Ereshkigal, crying out for what she has lost. In the end, when you emerge, you will be whole.

The descent is a return to yourself—a longing for who you were before your life made other plans.

Gentle Calls to Action

When my high school French teacher asked the class a question and no hands went up, she had a saying: "Voluntaire? Or Victime?" In other words, if you don't do it by choice, Madame Tucker-Houk is going to choose for you.

The descent is a necessary stage of becoming. Whether you choose the circumstances or life chooses for you, you can decide how to respond.

Begin to notice the small ways old patterns show up, and choose, in little moments, to respond differently. The shifts that matter most rarely happen in a single dramatic act. They happen in the quiet spaces, when you pause long enough to ask yourself what you truly want, and then honor the answer.

Notice your exhaustion without judgment. When you feel that familiar wave of weariness, instead of pushing it aside, try to listen. Ask yourself, "What is this tiredness trying to tell me?" Maybe it's pointing to the boundaries you've been avoiding. Maybe it's showing you the places where you give more than you receive. Maybe it's reminding you that you need rest, not another item checked off your to-do list.

Next, give yourself permission to say no. It doesn't have to be dramatic. It can be as simple as declining an invitation you don't actually want to accept or letting a task wait until tomorrow. Each time you say no, you create space for a deeper yes. You begin to show yourself that your time and energy matter.

Experiment with resting without guilt. Take a walk, sit in silence, read something purely for pleasure. Pay attention to the voice that insists you should be doing something "productive," and gently remind it that you are allowed to exist without earning it.

Practice speaking your truth in small, safe ways. Share an honest opinion when someone asks what you think. Admit when you don't know, or when you're not up for something. Notice how freeing it feels to let the truth come out without polishing it for someone else's comfort.

And finally, try extending kindness inward. You have been so well-trained to care for others that turning that care toward yourself may feel strange. But you deserve your own compassion. You deserve your own tenderness. Each time you soften toward yourself, you weaken the grip of the old story that said you had to be endlessly good in order to be worthy.

These aren't rules or assignments. They are gentle openings, invitations to begin shifting the way you move through the world. Take what resonates, leave the rest. There is no one right way to do this.

There is only the next brave step, however small, toward a life that feels like it belongs to you.

Ritual Suggestion

Choose a quiet evening when you won't be interrupted. Gather a small candle, a bowl of water, and something from nature—a stone, a flower, or a leaf you feel drawn to. Place them together in front of you, forming a simple altar. These elements represent fire, water, and earth—reminders of balance and wholeness.

Light the candle and take a few slow breaths. As you settle, place your hand over your heart and speak aloud: "I release the weight of being good. I invite the freedom of being whole." Repeat it three times, letting the words land in your body rather than just your mind.

Now dip your fingers into the water and gently touch your forehead, your throat, and your chest. With each touch, imagine yourself washing away the stories that told you to be quiet, to be small, to be pleasing above all else. See those stories dissolve like ink in water.

Finally, pick up your stone, flower, or leaf. Hold it in your palm and whisper one quality you want to bring forward instead—truth, rest, joy, power, or whatever arises for you. Let that word anchor into the object as a reminder of your commitment to yourself.

Blow out the candle, knowing that the flame lives on inside you. Keep the object somewhere you'll see it often, as a touchstone whenever you feel yourself slipping back into old patterns.

Journal Prompts

Take your time with these prompts. You don't need to answer them all at once. Let your pen move without editing or censoring, and trust that whatever comes up is what you're ready to see.

- What do I remember about being praised for being "good" as a child? How did it shape the way I learned to behave?
- Where in my life do I still measure my worth by how much I do for others? What feelings come up when I imagine stepping back from those roles?
- Think of a recent time when I felt drained, resentful, or overextended. What would it have looked like to honor my own limits in that moment?
- Write about a time when I said no, even if it was small. How did my body feel afterward? What did I learn about myself in that choice?
- If I could set down one expectation that no longer fits me, what would it be? What might become possible if I let it go?
- What is one word or phrase that captures what I most long to feel in this next chapter of my life?

As you reflect, notice any patterns that appear. Notice where your answers surprise you. These pages are not about judging yourself; they are about listening. The more you listen, the clearer your truth becomes.

When the Good Girl Rests

There comes a moment when you stop reaching for the next gold star. You stop looking for approval. You simply sit down. You let the mask slip. You breathe.

This isn't failure—it's arrival. When the Good Girl rests, the woman beneath her can rise. She finally remembers that she doesn't have to hustle for worthiness. She was worthy all along.

Chapter 2

The Space They Leave Behind

Loss rearranges us.

Sometimes it happens suddenly, with a phone call in the middle of the night or an empty chair at the table that will never be filled again.

Other times it happens slowly, like a friendship that fades without explanation, or a partner who withdraws little by little until you're both just going through the motions.

However it comes, loss always leaves a space. And while it hurts like hell, that space also offers an opportunity for transformation.

Watching our children become adults and strike out on their own is a common experience at this time. It is the end of a season—the daily rhythms, the background noise, the invisible purpose that shaped who we were for so long.

We pack their bags, smile for the photos, and tell them how proud we are, but something inside of us is breaking. There's a hole in our hearts the size and shape of the child we carried for so long. While they stand at the start of a grand adventure, we come home to empty days, quiet houses, and the deep sadness of feeling like we're no longer needed.

While we want nothing but the best for our children, we must take time to grieve this loss of purpose, to wander for a while, and to allow ourselves to be lost between worlds, unsure of who we are without someone to nurture. This is the space they leave behind, and it's up to us to allow that space to become a threshold that calls us back to ourselves.

Meet Demeter

A long time ago, when the gods of Olympus still shaped the lives of mortals, there lived Demeter, goddess of the harvest. Wherever she walked, the fields ripened and the orchards bowed heavy with fruit.

Demeter had a daughter, Persephone, who was bright and curious and carried the spirit of spring wherever she went. When Persephone wandered the meadows, flowers bloomed at her touch, and her laughter made the earth feel alive. To her mother, she was everything.

But not everyone who noticed Persephone was so pure of heart. Beneath her feet, Hades, god of the underworld, lived in a vast, shadowy kingdom. He was powerful, but lonely. One day, Hades looked up at the living world and saw Persephone. She was so beautiful, so alive, that his heart softened when he saw her. In that moment, he decided he wanted her by his side.

He knew Demeter would never allow it. So, Hades went to his brother Zeus, king of the gods, for permission. Zeus didn't exactly say yes, but he didn't say no either. That was all Hades needed.

One afternoon, Persephone wandered away from her friends, drawn to a flower unlike any other—a narcissus, glowing with unnatural beauty. When she bent to pick it, the ground split open beneath her feet. Out of the chasm thundered Hades in his black chariot, horses wild and sparking fire. Before she could cry out for her mother, he swept her into the underworld, and the earth closed above them.

When Persephone vanished, Demeter felt it immediately. She searched everywhere—across mountains and seas, calling her daughter's name until her voice broke. Finally, Hecate, the goddess of crossroads, whispered what had happened, and Helios, the sun, confirmed it: Hades had taken Persephone, and Zeus had allowed it.

Demeter's grief turned to rage. She abandoned her role as the goddess of the harvest. Crops failed, the earth went barren, and famine spread. People starved, and their cries finally reached Zeus. Fearing the collapse of the delicate balance between gods and mortals, he sent Hermes, his swift messenger, to demand Persephone's return.

Hades had no choice but to agree—but before he let her go, he offered Persephone a pomegranate. She ate a few seeds, not knowing the rule. Anyone who eats the food of the underworld can never fully leave it. (Didn't I say there's always a catch?)

When Hermes brought her back, Demeter embraced her daughter in relief, but her joy was short-lived. Because of the pomegranate, Persephone had to return to the underworld for half the year. While she was with her mother, Demeter's joy brought spring and summer to the earth. For the rest of the year, Persephone would return to the underworld, and during those months Demeter would grieve, and the world would fall into autumn and winter.

And that's how the seasons began—life and death, growth and decay, joy and sorrow, all woven together in Persephone's story. She became both the maiden of spring and the queen of the underworld, living in two worlds at once, reminding us that loss and return are part of the same cycle.

Mother and Child

If we set aside the kidnapping and obvious consent issues in this myth and consider it an allegory for children growing up and leaving home, then it's fair to say Demeter didn't handle this transition gracefully. She raged. She wept. She abandoned her fields and let the world go barren. For a time, her grief consumed everything she had once tended.

But in time, Demeter accepted that Persephone had become something new—no longer just her daughter, but queen of the underworld, powerful in her own right. That realization softened Demeter's sorrow. Although she missed her daughter terribly, she learned to live with the rhythm of absence and return. She began to understand that the love she had for her child didn't end. It just changed form. The descent asks the same of us.

I experienced this with my son, Samson. Those last few years went by so fast, and we talked openly about how the time had come for him to discover his own dreams. I tried to put a brave face on it, joking about how I couldn't wait for the endless emails from school to stop. But there was a deep ache, a longing for him to go back to the way he was, a baby-shaped hole in my heart.

Now, I can say I've successfully navigated the transition from boy-mom to man-mom. He is making his own way in the world, and it's amazing to see. When he needs me, and he still does sometimes, he knows where I am. Our reunions are joyful and always a little too short. I can't make the flowers bloom like Demeter, but sometimes it feels like I can.

When our children grow up and become fully independent, we can't go back to what was, but we can learn to appreciate and enjoy the new relationship that rises in its place. For me, this transition has been bittersweet, and sometimes I wish that little boy would come home. But only sometimes, because I am in awe of the thoughtful, responsible young man he's become.

Child and Mother

There's another side to this story—one that isn't addressed in the myth. What about Persephone? How did she feel about all this? Losing her mother must have felt like being torn from everything familiar. One moment she was gathering flowers in the sun; the next, she was swallowed by darkness, surrounded by strangers, expected to become queen of a world she never chose.

That's a pretty good description of what it feels like to lose a parent, which is another gate many of us walk through in midlife.

My mother and I had a difficult relationship. She was troubled, and I took on a lot of responsibilities that should not have fallen to me so early in life. Good Girl responsibilities, like protecting my sister and trying to manage Mom's emotions for her.

As an adult, I pulled back from mothering her, and she didn't like it. At the same time, her own demons seemed to get the upper hand more often. Most of our conversations spiraled into arguments. She didn't take much interest in my work or my family, but somehow it seemed like I was always letting her down, one way or another.

I remember one time I called her to check in.

"Well, nice of you to finally call," she said, with her trademark sarcasm.

"Yeah, I guess it's been a while," I said.

"Nineteen days."

Huh. That was like a long time. Still, life was busy. I was running my own business, and I had a toddler running around. I chuckled. "But who's counting, right?"

"I am," she replied.

A few years after I completed my cancer journey, Mom became seriously ill. She was a lifelong alcoholic and it had ravaged her body. At the age of 64, she looked to be at least 20 years older. Mom spent several years in and out of the hospital. Her decline was painful and prolonged—not a death I would wish on anyone. I wish she'd had a deathbed conversion, but the drinking and the arguments never stopped. I still found it difficult to spend time with her.

Finally, the day came. Mom was mostly unconscious by then. The hospital called us in for a meeting with the palliative care team.

"There isn't anything else we can do for her," the doctors said. "Multiple organ systems are failing. Every time we try to take her off the machines, she crashes."

It fell to me to explain all this to my dad, who was still convinced she was going to get better. That was one of the hardest and most important things I've ever done. After that, we went to her bedside to say goodbye.

Dad was devastated, and the next few weeks were a blur, helping him with the arrangements, answering delicate questions from well-meaning friends and family, and navigating his first Christmas without her in 40 years. There wasn't much room for me to grieve, at least not right away.

But there was a moment, a few weeks after she died, when I thought,

I should call Mom,

Then,

I can't.

She's gone.

She's really gone.

In that moment, grief opened up beneath my feet. I almost collapsed, barely steadying myself on the side of the bed. It hit so hard because, at that time, I believed that her death meant the difficulties between us could never be settled. I would never have the mother I wanted, because it was too late.

It was the permanence of the change that shook me to my core. And the realization that I was truly on my own for the first time.

And the Other One

Not all losses arrive through death or distance. Some of us also experience the quiet unraveling of a relationship we thought would last forever. The end of a marriage, or any lengthy partnership, can feel like a kind of death—a dismantling of the life you built together, piece by piece. This may or may not happen to you during midlife, but if it does, you are not alone.

There are a thousand ways this can go, but often it's the accumulation of unspoken grievances and resentments that have built up over time, only to burst forth during the descent. At least, that's what happened to me.

Early in our relationship, Dave and I talked about having children together, even though he was already 40 and had two sons who were 13 and 10 at the time. I told him I wanted two of my own, and he agreed. But getting pregnant was easier said than done. My body just wasn't getting the message. After five years of trying, we started fertility treatments.

Fertility treatments are no joke. I was only on the first rung of the ladder and I had to give myself hormone injections every day to ripen my eggs, then endure blood tests and vaginal ultrasounds every other day. Finally, they told me it was time, and I gave myself the magic "ovulate NOW!" injection. A day later, I conceived our son on a doctor's table with my feet in stirrups. Dave sat next to me, looking a bit bewildered. "Should we hold hands or something?" I asked. We laughed.

I didn't really expect to get pregnant on the first try, but a week later, sitting in the audience at a guitar concert, my inner knowing kicked in. There weren't any physical signs, but I was certain that I was pregnant. And I was right.

Being Samson's mom was a dream come true. I was clueless about how to take care of a baby, but Dave was a great dad and we muddled through. The first time my baby boy smiled at me, it took my breath away.

When he was almost two and a half, I told Dave I was ready to try for our second baby. He seemed less enthusiastic than before, but we each did our preliminary tests and I made the appointment for the first consultation.

Days before the appointment, I was diagnosed with breast cancer.

The diagnosis kicked off a flurry of visits with different specialists. I listened carefully to all the recommendations and answered any questions they had. But all I wanted to know was if I'd be able to have another baby after finishing treatment. And every time they told me they didn't know, Dave seemed a little more relieved.

Then came that day on the beach. My parents and sister were there. I had healed from my mastectomy and was rocking a swim prosthesis, which is a fake boob that you can wear in your bathing suit. Three-year-old Samson was napping on a blanket under the umbrella.

I was admiring his nap, as mothers do, why my own mother said something like, "Well, I guess that's the only grandchild I'm going to get."

I was horrified. "No mom," I said. "We're going to have another one."

Dave chuckled and said, "No, we're not."

I looked at him, confused.

"Of course we are," I said.

He looked back at me. "No, we're not."

And that's how my son's father told me that he had changed his mind about having another baby.

To be honest, I thought about leaving him right then and there. I did the math in my head. How long would it take to find someone else I wanted to have a baby with, who also wanted to have a baby with me? Samson was already three. Would it be fair to give him a little brother or sister when he was eight or nine? That wasn't what I envisioned for my family.

Then I thought about my son. Was I willing to put him through a divorce and growing up with a broken family, all in the name of a second child who was largely theoretical?

No, I was not.

So I swallowed it. The biggest dream I ever had was dead. And my marriage was on borrowed time.

It's never about one thing. But that one thing attracted other grievances like yellow jackets to a juicy watermelon. Maybe things would have been different if I'd said, "We need to talk about these swarming insects," but I never did. And neither did he.

It all broke loose during my descent, when I realized that my marriage wasn't serving any of us. I started saving money, making plans, holding on as long as I could. In the end, I didn't leave for another baby. That ship had sailed. I left for me, and for the dreams that were still inside me. I knew that staying would mean shrinking myself to fit into a too-small life. That wasn't the ending I wanted, and it wasn't the example I wanted to set for our son.

Leaving—or being left—reshapes you. Even if the decision is mutual, it cuts deep. You lose not just the person, but the story you told about who you were together. That's why the space they leave behind feels so hollow at first. Because it's up to you to decide who you are now.

Who Are You Now?

Remember Inanna's golden ring? Removing it required her to surrender all the relationships and promises that once defined her. In surrender, some of your relationships will end, and some will change. This is your opportunity to redefine who you are. Who are you when the roles that once defined you—mother, daughter, wife—fall away?

It's a frightening question, but also a sacred one. Because in the absence of those identities, you meet yourself again. You rediscover the woman who existed before she learned to compromise and accommodate. You remember what she loved, what made her laugh, what lit her up from the inside. You begin to build a new rhythm, one that belongs only to you.

In the myth of Demeter and Persephone, the descent into darkness was not the end. It was the turning point. The same is true for us. The ending or transformation of a relationship, no matter how painful, can become a passage to deeper truth. The space left behind is not barren; it is fertile ground. It's where you begin again, where you plant new seeds of belonging, not to another person, but to yourself.

You may not know what's next. That's okay. Just as the earth rests in winter, your soul needs time to rest and remember. So trust that the life you're meant to live will emerge from the quiet. Even the things that end are part of your becoming.

Gentle Calls to Action

When something or someone leaves our lives, our instinct is to fill the emptiness as quickly as we can. We want the ache to stop, the silence to be broken. But healing doesn't come from hurrying. It comes from learning to be with what remains, and to let the space itself become a teacher. These calls to action are not about fixing. They are about slowing down enough to notice what's true and allowing that truth to soften you.

Begin by giving yourself permission to acknowledge the absence. Say their name out loud. Write it on paper. Walk into the room that feels too empty and just stand there. Sometimes the kindest thing you can do for yourself is to stop pretending it doesn't hurt. Naming the reality that something or someone is missing is an important step.

Try creating a ritual of remembrance. Light a candle, place a photograph on a table, or cook a meal they loved. If the space comes from a life change rather than a death, honor that too. Write a letter to the part of yourself that belonged to that role or season. Thank her for what she carried, and let her know you see her. Marking transitions, even in small ways, helps us move with them rather than against them.

Practice letting the empty space be empty. Instead of filling every hour with distractions, allow yourself to sit quietly. Notice what comes up. It might be grief, or anger, or longing. It might be relief. Whatever it is, let it exist without rushing to change it. These feelings are part of your story. They will shift in their own time.

Look for traces of presence in the absence. What memories surface when you pause? What qualities or lessons live on in you because of who or what has gone? Write them down or speak them aloud. Often, we find that love does not end with loss. It simply takes on a new form.

Finally, hold on to the possibility that new life can emerge from the empty places. You don't have to know what it will look like yet. You don't have to force anything to happen. Just trust that the space itself is fertile. Like a winter field, it may look barren now, but beneath the surface, something is preparing to grow.

Ritual Suggestion

Choose a quiet time when you can be alone. Gather a candle, a small bowl, and a loose piece of paper. Sit somewhere that feels safe and still. Place the unlit candle and the bowl in front of you.

Close your eyes and take several slow, deep breaths. Allow yourself to think of the person, role, or season that is no longer with you. Notice the feelings that rise. Let them come without judgment.

When you're ready, write down what you miss most. It may be a name, a memory, a daily routine, or a word that captures the loss. Fold the paper gently and place it in the bowl. Speak aloud, "I honor what has been. I acknowledge the space that remains."

Now light the candle. Watch its flame. Imagine it carrying your words upward, holding them in light. Let the flame remind you that, even in absence, something continues—love, memory, influence, possibility. Sit with the candle for a few minutes, breathing slowly, feeling both the ache and the warmth.

When you're ready, you may choose to keep the paper tucked somewhere safe, or bury it in the earth as a gesture of planting something new. Blow out the candle with gratitude, knowing the ritual is complete.

This simple act marks the space left behind as sacred, reminding you that grief and growth can live side by side.

Journal Prompts

Take these prompts gently, one at a time. Let your pen move slowly and honestly. There are no right answers, only the truths that rise in the moment.

- What loss or ending feels most present in me right now? What words would I use to describe the space it has left behind?
- When I think of the person, role, or season that is gone, what do I miss most? What do I carry forward?
- How have I tried to fill the emptiness? Has it brought me comfort, or has it deepened my sadness?
- Write about a memory that still feels alive within me. What does it reveal about the love or meaning that remains even after the loss?
- What emotions have I avoided allowing myself to feel? If I gave those feelings a voice on the page, what would they say?
- Imagine that the empty space is fertile soil. If something new were to grow there, what might it be?

As you write, don't rush. Let yourself linger in both the ache and the possibility. The space left behind is not a void to escape, but a quiet place that invites reflection. Step into it with tenderness, honor what has been, and listen for what might be waiting to emerge.

The Space Is an Invitation

The places that feel most hollow in our lives are often the very places where transformation begins. We can't bring back what has been lost, and we can't return to who we were before. But we can choose to honor the absence rather than deny it. We can let the space remain open, tender, and alive, trusting that it will shape us into someone new.

Like Inanna rising from the underworld, we do not come back unchanged. We carry the memory of what is gone and the wisdom of what remains. The space they leave behind is not an ending, but a threshold. And on the other side of that threshold, life waits to meet us again.

Chapter 3

The Body Remembers

"This is a waste of my time. There are half a dozen other tests you should have first."

I perched on the edge of the stiff waiting room sofa, bare arms and legs pressed against my body, blinking at her. Then I shifted my weight and the paper gown made a crinkling sound.

The technician scoffed and stormed down the hallway, leaving me alone.

In the corner, rumpled magazines spilled over the edges of a small table. I reached for a copy of *The New Yorker* and started to read.

For as long as I could remember, words could be counted upon. When life was at its bleakest, they sheltered me in the narrow spaces between them. I could escape into the folds of a book any time I wanted, and I wanted to escape all the time.

Like now, for instance.

But the words failed me. They streamed through my eyeballs, missing my brain and sticking in the back of my throat, unread.

Then she was back.

The technician's demeanor had changed completely. "Okay honey," she said softly. "Come with me."

I followed her into an exam room, eyeing the machinery the way an awkward teenager sizes up the popular boys in the cafeteria.

The technician pecked at the keyboard with ebony fingers. Her scrubs were covered in a vague floral pattern. She had very large breasts. I wondered how she fit them into the machine.

She pressed the enter key, then spun on her stool to face me. "Okay," she said, "let's see what you've got."

A little while later, I returned to my post on the waiting room sofa, arms crossed and eyes squeezed shut against the clamor of the busy radiology office. My breasts ached. I crossed and recrossed my bare legs and wondered for the tenth time why they couldn't be bothered to provide real gowns.

The mammogram tech reappeared. "She wants to do an ultrasound," she said.

'She' must be the radiologist, I thought. I followed the technician down the hall, where she handed me off to a petite Hispanic woman with a soft accent. The woman told me her name, and I immediately forgot it. Two turns later, we stepped into the ultrasound room.

"This is where I had my ultrasound when I was pregnant with my son," I said. I couldn't help but smile at the memory.

"Is it? We'll try to get you out of here as quickly as we can."

"He's two," I said, sliding onto the table.

The woman did not answer, so I busied myself by counting the tiles in the ceiling.

Forty-five minutes later, I wiped ultrasound goo from my breasts and changed into a new paper gown. The radiology tech led me to a different waiting area.

Everything had gone quiet. Men and women in scrubs scurried past, but no one spoke. No one looked me in the eye.

Much later, I realized that I was the only person in radiology that day who did not know I had breast cancer.

My body and I have never been on good terms. I was bullied continuously as a child because I was overweight and, let's face it, weird. In high school, I had terrible acne. When I was 22, I was diagnosed with fibromyalgia. You already know about the fertility treatments. And now...

I was 33 years old. No family history.

This should not have happened to me.

But it did.

The day after the biopsy, while we were still waiting for results, my general practitioner called me. The one who couldn't help but twitch when she squeezed my nipple and blood came out. She asked me if I had any questions.

"The only question I have is the one you can't answer. Do I have breast cancer?"

She paused. Too long.

"I can tell you that we don't see symptoms like yours in women who do *not* have breast cancer."

I ended the call, and then I fell apart. Sobbing on the bathroom floor. Unable to stop thinking about who would raise my son.

Then I had a thought that changed everything. It pulled me back together and allowed me to power through my illness with grim determination. Can you guess what it was?

I got cancer because I'm strong enough to bear it. Because of me, someone else—someone who can't cope—won't have to go through this.

At the time, I thought I was a superhero. Now, in the context of the descent, I recognize it as the ultimate good girl move. It kept me going, but at what cost? I held cancer at arm's length. Compartmentalized it. And, because of this, I missed the message.

How would my life have unfolded if I'd stayed in uncertainty? What would have happened if I'd allowed myself to consider the questions that were bubbling up inside of me? Who was I being in the years leading up to my diagnosis? Was I being true to myself? What if I stopped trying to live up to other people's expectations and started doing what I *wanted* to do? What would happen if I took off my armor and showed up differently—more authentic, more vulnerable, more real?

These questions pointed to the lesson my cancer was trying to teach me. But I ignored them. Stuffed them deep down inside my body, along with all my terror and sadness. I kept on going, just like I always did. The good girl, the strong one, the one who didn't need anybody.

What I didn't know then was that my entire life, my body had been trying to protect me. It took my fear and rage and shame and walled it off inside—just because I asked it to. It dragged along behind me while I operated entirely in my head. Soon, my body had become nothing more than a dumping ground for all the pain I'd endured.

The body remembers what we have tried to forget. It carries the imprints of our earliest fears, the patterns of our families, the griefs we never named, and even the joys that slipped by unacknowledged. Long before we have words for what has happened to us, our bodies are writing the story.

But that can't go on forever. In my case, something had to give. My body needed me to wake up. To stop criticizing her for being too big, too round, too soft. To stop punishing her with short lived, crazy diets and bouts of extreme exercise. To feel the emotions that had been trapped inside. Instead, I ignored the blaring alarms and carried on as I always had, doubling down on the stress and self-loathing that had created this monster in the first place.

I survived the cancer, but missed the lesson, which was to remember I had a body, and that she deserved my loving presence. That I deserved my loving presence.

But you always get another chance.

During the descent, if we allow it, our bodies will lead us back to truth. The body remembers, and in its remembering, it offers a way home.

Don't take my word for it. Ask the Selkie.

Meet the Selkie

A long time ago, on a rugged coast where the sea met the cliffs, there lived creatures who could slip between worlds. They were called selkies—seal folk. They shed their skins under the light of the moon and walked the shore as women.

One night, a fisherman saw a selkie dancing on the rocks. She was radiant, her hair shining like wet silk, her laughter carried on the wind. She carefully laid her seal skin on the rocks to wade into the tide pools. Moved by a strange longing, he crept forward, took the skin, and hid it in his home.

When the selkie returned to the rocks and saw her skin was gone, she panicked. She searched the shore until dawn, but could not find it. When dawn came, she tried to reenter the sea, but it no longer recognized her.

The man came out from his hiding place and offered her warmth and safety, a home on land, a life she could grow into. She was desperate, so she followed him home.

And she stayed.

In time, she learned to live like a woman. She bore his children. She baked bread and tended the fire. She smiled when neighbors passed by and said she was lucky to have such a kind husband. But her eyes always drifted toward the horizon. Every night she dreamed of saltwater and waves. Every morning she woke with sand between her fingers.

The body remembers what the mind tries to forget.

Years passed before she found it—the hidden bundle tucked behind the flour sacks, still smelling faintly of the sea. Her breath caught. Her pulse quickened. The moment her hands touched the slick pelt, she knew there was no going back to pretending.

That night, while her family slept, she slipped from the house and walked barefoot toward the waves. The sea opened its arms, and she dove beneath the surface. They say the children sometimes saw her afterward, a dark shape in the surf, watching from a distance. They say she never forgot them.

And the sea never forgot her.

The Skin We Shed

Like the Selkie, we are born in wild waters—whole, intuitive and alive. But somewhere along the way, we learn to live on land. To trade our skin for belonging. To push down the instincts that rise when something isn't right.

We smile, we serve, we perform. We say yes when our bodies are screaming no. We keep the peace at all costs. And little by little, the life we were meant to live recedes like a tide pulling back from the shore.

But the body remembers.

It remembers the rhythm of the waves and the taste of salt. It remembers the skin you once wore—the one that fit perfectly before you were told never to let it show.

Sometimes remembering arrives as exhaustion, pain or illness. Sometimes it's a quiet knowing that the life you've built no longer fits. Either way, the body speaks the language of the soul. It is the keeper of everything you've ever seen or done and every voice you've ever silenced, especially your own.

Like the Selkie, you don't have to ask permission to come home to yourself. Begin simply, by listening. Each deep breath, each moment of rest, each honest no is a way of reaching for your skin again.

Your body has not betrayed you. It has been protecting you, holding the grief, rage, joy and longing you weren't ready to feel. It has been waiting for you to remember.

When you do, something ancient stirs. The tide begins to turn. The current of your life carries you back toward what's real.

Learning to Listen

My cancer treatment consisted of six rounds of chemotherapy followed by a mastectomy. The first chemo treatment went fine. Afterward, we went for kebabs and I ate my whole dish. At 4:00 am I puked every last grain of rice into the kitchen sink. I lost 10 pounds in three days.

My oncologist said, "It sounds like if we can just get this nausea under control, you'll be fine." He gave me steroids to take for three days before my next infusion. The steroids prevented me from sleeping, so I used the extra time to paint my dining room.

Through it all I kept working. A client said, "I can't believe how you're staying so positive." I replied, "What good would it do to curl up in the corner and cry?"

Anti-emetics. Sleeping pills. White blood cell boosters. At one point I had 13 prescriptions and 10 of them were for side effects. I had to make a chart to keep track of them all. I told my sister, "Cancer is like getting a second job, but the hours are terrible and you can't stop puking."

After my third infusion, they sent me to a therapist. He asked me how I was doing, and I told him I was annoyed I'd missed a few deadlines.

He asked me what would happen if I just stopped working, took time for myself, went outside and chased butterflies with my son? I laughed at him.

Stopping was the furthest thing from my mind. If I did, what would happen then? If I kept going, I'd never have to find out.

My last chemo treatment was on my birthday. I made pink cupcakes with sprinkles and handed them out to the nurses and the other patients.

In January, I had my mastectomy. It hurt less than I thought it would. The worst part was emptying the drains. Afterward, my surgeon told me they tested 17 lymph nodes and they were all negative.

My oncologist said he didn't think I should have reconstruction, so I didn't. Then he said he thought I should get radiation, so I made an appointment for a consult.

Five days a week for eight weeks. Can't miss a day. No problem. I show up. That's what I do. She started down the list of side effects and then...

"...spontaneous rib fracture..."

"Sorry, what?"

"I said, 'spontaneous rib fracture,'" she repeated.

"I heard what you said. But...are you saying I could be walking around my house three years from now and a rib will just...break?"

"Yes, that's what I'm saying."

I paused. For the first time since I got my diagnosis.

"I have to think about it," I said.

I made an appointment with my surgeon. He'd always been straight with me.

"What can I do for you?" he asked.

"I need to run something by you."

"Okay, shoot."

"I don't want to get the radiation. I need you to tell me if I'm being crazy."

He said something next that I will never forget.

"Look, you're an anomaly. There's no data on people like you. Suppose you don't get the radiation. If your cancer comes back in five years, everyone will say, 'You should have gotten the radiation.' If it doesn't, everyone will say, 'You were smart not to get the radiation.' The bottom line is, nobody knows, so you have to trust your gut."

When he said, "trust your gut," what he was really saying was listen to your body.

My body was telling me that it had been through enough. That those 17 lymph nodes meant something. That the cancer was gone.

I listened. And 15 years later, I'm still cancer free. No radiation required.

This is not about whether radiation is good or bad. I'm not giving you medical advice. I'm telling you that your body has wisdom that you cannot begin to fathom. I'm urging you to listen.

Remembering the Body

My body. Long before my cancer diagnosis, it had been a source of pain and rejection. It brought me nothing but unwanted attention and constant bullying, at home and at school. And so I left it behind, like the Selkie.

By the time I was 30 I had completely dissociated from it. To me, it barely existed. I had no sense of how big or small it was, how it functioned, or how I looked naked. I never looked—really looked—at myself in the mirror. My body had been reduced to a few features that had to be "fixed" before I considered myself presentable: a mane of hair, dark eyelashes, and a number on the scale.

Cancer took my hair. Then it took my eyelashes. It disrupted my weight so much that the number on the scale became meaningless. And just like that, all my filters were gone.

My greatest fear was that one day my son would pull my hair and come away a fistful. So I decided to shave my head before that became a possibility.

Afterward, I didn't go straight home. I went to a nearby park and hiked to a place I knew along the shore of a lake. I had knotted the bandanna before I even got out of the stylist's chair. Now as I sat, alone, the lake lapping the shore at my feet, I reached up and pulled off that bandanna. I touched my bare scalp, tentatively at first, as if I expected it to hurt. For the next half hour I got acquainted with my own head. And I cried.

At home, I looked in the mirror and saw my face—really saw it—for the first time in years. I looked into my own eyes, and I felt all the shame that I'd hidden inside for so long. I thought it would destroy me. But it made me stronger.

A few months later, another insult. Cancer took my breast. I was afraid to look at first. I kept myself covered with the surgical bra they'd wrapped around me in recovery. At my first follow-up appointment, my surgeon carefully covered all my wounds in plastic. "Now you can take a shower," he said. I craved and dreaded it in equal measure.

At home, I removed my clothes slowly, like I was preparing for my own execution. I stood in front of the bathroom mirror and tore the velcro on the front of the surgical bra. I didn't know what I would feel. But I was as numb as the scar that ran across my chest.

A week later, I received the pathology report. In it, the pathologist described the shape and color of my nipple. I thought, *how strange that my nipple—the nipple I'd used to feed my child—should be sitting on his table, far away from me.*

My body had come apart. It existed only in pieces. And even though I'd paid no attention to it for years, in that moment, I wanted all the pieces back. I wanted to be reassembled, like Humpty Dumpty after his great fall. But not even all the king's men could accomplish that feat.

Life went on, as it does. I moved through the world without my missing pieces. My eyelashes grew back, and so did my hair, although much grayer than before. The steroids, which protected me from that terrible nausea, caused the extra pounds to come back, and then some.

I ordered my breast prosthesis and had my bras altered to hold it in place. My body felt more unreal than ever.

Years passed. I told myself I would get reconstruction once I had lost the weight. But no matter what I did, it would not come off.

Then one day, at the end of another brutal group exercise class, our coach said, "Friends, I want you to think of the one thing you've been putting off. The one thing you have told yourself you would do when your body was perfect. And I want you to decide to do it. Not then, but right now. Don't wait any longer."

The next day I made an appointment with my surgeon to talk about reconstruction.

All that time, I didn't realize how much the loss of my breast had affected my confidence and my sense of self. I told myself it was just a breast, an extra piece I no longer needed. But when I got it back, everything changed. Like the day I shaved my head, I saw myself again for the first time. And I recognized me.

That was the true ending of my cancer journey. The day I became whole was the day I began to heal. It was the day I saw myself with new eyes.

The loss of the physical body, or at least your idea of it, is an important stage of the descent. It can feel like hanging from the meat hook in Ereshkigal's throne room, whether for three days like Inanna, or six years, like me. After all that, remembering the body feels like coming home.

Gentle Calls to Action

The Selkie reminds us that coming home to ourselves isn't about doing more. It's about listening more deeply to the small signals we've spent a lifetime overriding. These invitations are not tasks or fixes. They are simple ways to come back to the language of your own body.

Begin by noticing what your body is saying. Pause throughout the day and ask, What is true right now? You might sense tension in your jaw, a flutter in your belly, or an opening in your chest. Don't rush to interpret or change anything. Just notice. Awareness is the first step in remembering your skin.

When someone asks something of you—your time, your energy, your care—pause before answering. Feel for the subtle response inside. A true yes expands. A false yes contracts. Let this awareness guide you when responding to requests, even the small ones.

Give yourself what you once denied. If your body wants rest, let it rest. If it wants movement, stretch or walk. If it craves touch, warmth, water, or laughter, give it those things without guilt. Every act of care tells the body, *I'm listening now.*

Soften the armor you've built over time. Many of us carry invisible shields of tension, politeness, or productivity. Notice where you hold yours—shoulders, belly, back, smile—and breathe into that place. Let it loosen a little bit at a time. The more softness you allow, the more truth can move through you.

Remember that healing is cyclical. Like the tides that call the Selkie home, the process of remembering ebbs and flows. Some days you'll feel wild and free. Others, you'll feel like you've lost your skin again. That's okay. Each return to yourself strengthens the bond between body and soul.

Ritual Suggestion

This ritual is simple but powerful: it's an act of returning.

Find a quiet moment, near water if you can—a bath, a creek, the ocean, even the kitchen sink will do. Place your hands in the water and close your eyes. Take three slow breaths.

As you breathe, imagine the parts of yourself that have been silenced or hidden. The one who smiled when she wanted to cry. The one who said yes when she longed to say no. The one who worked until her body ached just to feel worthy.

Now whisper softly, "I remember you. I'm bringing you home."

Let the water hold those words. Let it remind you that you are fluid and resilient, made for movement and change. When you're ready, lift your hands from the water, touch them to your heart, and whisper, "I am home in this body. I am safe here."

Repeat as often as needed. Every time you do, a piece of your true skin comes back.

Journal Prompts

These prompts are invitations to speak with your body as you would an old friend. Take your time. Write slowly and savor the discovering.

- What messages has my body been trying to send me lately? What sensations, pains, or cravings might be asking for attention?
- Where do I feel "tight" in my life—physically or emotionally? What might that tightness be protecting?

- When do I feel most alive in my body? What am I doing, and who am I with?
- How have I silenced my body's truth to please others or keep the peace?
- What would it look like to reclaim my own rhythm? What pace, rest, and nourishment feels right for me?
- If my body could speak without fear of judgment, what would it say?

Write without censoring. Let your body answer through you. You may be surprised by how much it remembers.

The Truth Beneath the Skin

The Selkie's story is not about escape—it's about return. Her freedom was never something new to earn; it was something old to remember.

The same is true for you.

Your body has never forgotten who you are. Beneath the layers of performance and politeness, beneath the good girl mask and the striving, there is a rhythm that has always been yours. It is patient. It is ancient. It is waiting.

Each time you breathe deeply, rest honestly, or speak a truth you used to swallow, you call another piece of yourself back from the shore.

The body remembers. And through it, you can find your way home.

Part Two

Initiation

Be still and know. Stop fleeing. Stop pleasing. Stop ignoring your knowing. Stop pretending. There is a voice of knowing inside each woman. The way home is to hear her.

Glennon Doyle

Dave and I were together for 18 years. That's a pretty good run, especially with everything we'd been through together.

He has a story about our marriage and how it ended. So do I. Mine is that neither of us was a particularly good communicator, and we found it impossible to talk about hard things. For this reason, resentments built up until they were so big and so explosive, we couldn't possibly resolve them.

I don't know what his story is. I haven't asked, and he wouldn't tell me even if I did. That's okay. His story is not my problem.

Logistically, it went like you'd expect. First, I moved into the guest bedroom. I spent a lot of time away from home. We passed each other like ships in the night.

One morning, I had to drop my car off for repairs, and he picked me up. We hadn't had a real conversation in weeks. Hadn't even been in the same room.

"Is there any chance we're going to get back together?" he asked.

"No," I replied.

"Then I need you to move out. It's too painful with you in the house."

I just nodded. When we got home, I went to work on the problem.

I'm a fast mover. Once I make a decision, I don't spend a bunch of time agonizing over it. I called the closest apartment complex and made an appointment to see a place that same day. Two days after that, my application was approved and my move-in date was set. It took me less than two weeks to move out.

That first night in my apartment was bliss. It was nothing compared to the house I had lived in with Dave, but it was mine. Samson was 11. He had stayed with his Dad, but he was less than a mile away. He had a bedroom at my place, and he could come and go as he pleased.

I remember sitting on the living room floor that first night, unpacking my books. It was quiet. Too quiet. I turned on the television and let the voices wash over me. It felt wrong. I turned the television off again. I needed to get used to the quiet. Needed to probe its corners for lessons I couldn't fathom while I was spiraling under the weight of everything that was not mine.

It wasn't comfortable, but it felt true. I was finally free.

The Great Pause

There comes a moment, after the unraveling, when the silence settles. For me, it was that first night in my own place.

I had surrendered a lot. I had stopped caring about what others thought about me. I had lost my mother and ended my marriage. I had been to hell and back, thanks to an improbable cancer diagnosis. All those losses, but I'd never felt more whole.

The descent loosens what no longer belongs. Initiation asks us to pause in the space that's left. It's the middle ground, the in-between. Not the old story, not yet the new. It is where you learn to dwell with yourself without distraction, without masks, and without the performance of survival.

I was living alone for the first time in more than 15 years. I was in the pause, and it was hushed, like a cathedral on a Tuesday afternoon.

At first, the stillness feels strange. We're used to filling the void with tasks and people, with busyness and noise. We scroll our phones. We clean the kitchen. We pile on new projects. Anything to avoid the silence. Because silence speaks, and we don't always like what it has to say.

That voice is not a critic, though it may feel sharp at first. It's not a taskmaster, though it may call on you to act differently. It's the voice of your own knowing, the one that has been with you since childhood, the one you learned to ignore to survive.

Initiation is the process of learning to hear her again.

Remembering the Girl

Part of the initiation is remembering who you were before the world told you who to be. The girl who loved horses. The girl who wrote stories late at night under the covers. The girl who believed in magic. She was still inside of me.

When I was 15, I went on an exchange trip to France. My exchange student's name was Sabrine. I was excited to meet her because she told me that she loved riding horses. I hadn't ridden in a few years, but I was sure we would have so much in common.

While I was staying with her and her family in Pornic, she took me along to her riding lesson. I was nervous. I thought I'd be rusty, but my body remembered what to do. I didn't understand what the instructor was saying, but I tried to follow along with what the other students were doing. Then we started to canter.

There is nothing in the world that feels like confidently cantering around on a horse. It's like a dance, your hips moving with the horse's rhythm, your breath with their breath. You are no longer a human on a horse. You and your horse are one. It had been so long since I'd felt that. It felt like I could ride forever.

These are the memories that come to you during your initiation—flashes of the moments when you felt most alive. Not when you were achieving, not when you were pleasing, but when you were simply being your true self. These memories are clues. They point toward what your soul has always known.

Remembering the girl is not about recreating the past. It's about recovering the essence of who you've always been.

Claiming the Quiet

In a world that rewards noise, claiming quiet is radical. It is saying no to the endless demands of productivity and yes to the rhythm of your own spirit.

Quiet doesn't mean emptiness. Quiet is fertile. It's the ground where wisdom sprouts. But you can't hear the whisper of your soul if you're always drowning in noise.

My initiation began a year and a half before the COVID-19 pandemic strangled the world. We all learned a good deal about the quiet during that time, whether we wanted to or not.

During my own initiation, I learned to tune in to what I wanted. I moved through life at my own pace. Slowly, I began to let go of my need to control everyone and everything. I started to go with the flow of life and let the world move through me.

These small acts taught me that quiet is not wasted time. Quiet is where the answers live.

Inviting the Magic Back In

When you allow quiet to expand, space opens for magic. Like the synchronicities that arrive when you're paying attention, the symbols and dreams that guide you, or the wonder of being in rhythm with life.

I adopted a mantra during my initiation: *expect miracles*. I posted it on my refrigerator where I would see it every day. As I opened to the magic all around me, things I wanted but believed I could not have—even things I'd forgotten about—started showing up. Like true love. Spaciousness. Souls that were meant to guide me. During quiet contemplation, I finally understood what I came here to do, which laid the foundation for my life's work.

Initiation is about remembering that life isn't just tasks and obligations, to-do lists and bills. There's a vast mystery that's unfurling around you in every moment. You've just been too caught up in your own performance to see it.

What's Coming Up

In the next three chapters, we'll walk together through the tender middle ground of initiation—the pause between who you've been and who you're becoming. Each chapter invites you to listen more deeply, remember more fully, and let the quiet do its healing work.

In Chapter 4, we'll reconnect with the parts of ourselves we left behind. Those forgotten selves hold keys to our present wholeness. We'll listen for the voice of the girl within and begin to bring her gifts forward, not as relics of the past but as living threads in the woman you are now.

In Chapter 5, we'll explore practices of stillness and presence, learning to trust the fertile ground of silence. You'll discover how to rest in the in-between. How to stop pushing for answers and allow the next chapter of your life to reveal itself in its own time.

In Chapter 6, we'll invite wonder back in, weaving ritual, creativity, and synchronicity into our daily lives. Together, we'll remember that life is not just something to be managed, it's a conversation between your soul and the world.

Invitation

The unraveling has left you with space. Now it's time to rest within that space, to listen, and to let the voice of your knowing rise again. This isn't a season for striving. It's a season for receiving.

Don't be afraid of the quiet. The compass you've been looking for is there. Trust it. Follow it. Let it remind you that you're never alone, and that the magic of your own life is waiting to be discovered.

Chapter 4

Remembering the Girl

There were two things I loved as a girl. One was horses, and the other was writing.

When I was in fifth grade, a teacher took me aside and asked me about a poem I'd written. It was called "Larasa," and it was, unsurprisingly, about a horse I knew.

In those days, I wished every day were Saturday, when I would pull on my jodhpurs and tall, black rubber boots and splash through mud and manure to the stable. There were so many horses I loved there. Stocky, trusted schooling horses who knew how to take care of a gangly, uncoordinated girl like me.

Larasa was different. She was a gray Arabian mare—a slight, high-spirited horse who dazzled with beauty and grace. Every week I secretly hoped my teacher would let me ride her, but I was always disappointed. She was delicate and subtle, and I was...not.

No one had ever singled me out as a writer before, so when this teacher asked me about my poem, which was a love letter to Larasa, all I could say was, "She's real, and I love her so much."

"I can tell she's real," the teacher replied. And that was probably the greatest compliment I'd ever received in my life.

The thing I loved most about writing was the same thing I loved about reading—the feeling of slipping between the words and losing track of everything that was going on around me.

I didn't know it then, but that was my first taste of what it means to remember the girl—to be so absorbed in something you love that you forget to perform. Psyche's story begins in that same place: a girl whose beauty drew the world's attention, until she lost herself trying to be worthy of love again.

Meet Psyche

There was once a girl named Psyche, whose beauty was said to outshine even the goddess of love herself. People couldn't help but stare. They began bringing her the gifts that were intended for Aphrodite's temple.

You can imagine how that went over. The goddess was furious. So she sent her son, Eros, to make Psyche fall in love with the ugliest man alive.

But love doesn't always follow orders. Eros snuck into Psyche's chamber at night, arrow in hand—the kind that makes people fall in love with terrible matches. But as he bent over her, Psyche stirred in her sleep. Startled, he scratched himself with the arrow. And so he was caught in his own trap.

Instead of cursing her as his mother demanded, he carried her to a hidden palace where every need was met, every room glowed with unseen magic, and every night, a husband came to her in the dark, asking only that she never look upon his face.

For a while, she was happy. She felt cherished, even without knowing who he was. But her sisters planted seeds of doubt: "What if he's a monster?" they whispered.

So one night, Psyche lit a lamp and held it over his sleeping form. What she saw was not a monster, but Eros himself, radiant and divine. And in that moment of awe, a single drop of oil spilled from her lamp and burned his shoulder. He woke and, heartbroken, he disappeared.

That's where Psyche's real journey began.

Aphrodite told Psyche her husband would be restored to her after she completed four tasks. But Aphrodite was just toying with her. The tasks were impossible for any mortal to complete.

The first was to sort an enormous pile of seeds—barley, lentils, poppy, and millet—by nightfall. Psyche was overwhelmed and crumpled next to the heap in tears. But then, a colony of ants came to help, carrying each tiny seed to its place.

The second task was to collect golden fleece from dangerous rams with horns like knives. As she hid in the brush by the river, trying in vain to develop a plan, a gentle reed told her to wait until the heat of midday, when the rams rested, and then to gather the tufts caught on the thorn bushes. To her surprise, it worked.

The third task was even more impossible than the last. She was told to fetch water from the black river Styx, one of the rivers of the underworld. The water was sacred, dark, and deadly. It tumbled down cliffs so steep and sharp that no mortal could climb them. And it was guarded by dragons who scorched the air with fire. Psyche could not see how she could ever complete the task. But Zeus's eagle came to her aid, filling her cup and returning it safely to her hands.

Finally, Aphrodite sent Psyche to the underworld to retrieve a box of "beauty" from Persephone herself. Psyche followed the instructions given by the whispering stones: carry two coins for the ferryman, two cakes for the three-headed dog, speak to no one, and whatever you do—don't open the box.

She made it all the way back to the living world. But as she stood in the sunlight, box in hand, she thought, *Maybe I should take just a little. Maybe if I were more beautiful, he'd love me again.*

So she opened the box. And out came, not beauty, but a heavy, deathlike sleep.

Eros found her lying there, and his love had not dimmed. He lifted her up, brushed the dark sleep from her skin, and kissed her. At his kiss, she breathed again. Eros carried her to Olympus and pleaded with Zeus to make her immortal.

Some say Zeus acted out of respect for Eros. Some say he was amused at the chaos love always causes, or that he felt genuine compassion for Psyche's perseverance. Whatever the reason, he called the gods together and declared that Psyche had earned her place among them.

And, like the true mother-in-law she was, Aphrodite had no choice but to begrudgingly accept their union.

The Four Tasks of Remembering the Girl

Each of Aphrodite's trials held a hidden invitation for Psyche—not to prove her worth or earn back love, but to remember who she was before fear, shame, and striving took over.

Every challenge peeled away one more layer of what she had been told she must be, until only her truest self remained. That's the heart of remembering the girl: returning to the version of yourself who already knew how to trust, listen, and belong to herself.

Sorting the Seeds – Remembering Clarity

When Psyche faced that enormous mountain of seeds, she fell to her knees and wept. There was no way she could finish it on her own.

But when she finally stopped struggling, the ants came. They moved patiently through the pile, sorting each seed into its rightful place.

Can you remember a time when you fought hard for something that stubbornly refused to happen—only to discover that, once you stopped pushing, the right thing unfolded on its own? Maybe you didn't get what you thought you wanted, but instead received what you actually needed.

Remembering the girl begins this way—not by erasing her fire, but by teaching her when to rest. The girl within you knows how to want fiercely, how to stamp her foot and say "mine." But she's also learning that not everything can be claimed by force. When she grows quiet, she discovers another kind of power—the patience to let life show her what belongs.

This is the stage of quiet sorting: what's mine to carry, and what can I finally set down? The wisdom of the ants reminds us that clarity comes in small moments, through trust and gentleness, not through pushing harder.

Gathering the Golden Fleece – Remembering Timing

Once we've learned to pause and see what truly belongs to us, the next lesson is knowing when to act and when not to.

The girl within you is curious and brave, but she's also learning that not every challenge is meant to be charged into headfirst. Some things shimmer with danger disguised as opportunity. When you stop forcing and start listening, you begin to sense the rhythm underneath it all—the quiet invitation that says *wait now, go later*.

This is discernment, the wisdom to let the world meet you halfway. Not every victory comes from striving. Some come from standing still long enough to see where the path opens on its own.

The opposite of discernment is impulsiveness, and my impulsiveness is off the charts. I do the thing, usually in the most awkward, boorish way possible, and ask questions later. Sometimes that works for me and sometimes it leaves me feeling exhausted and stretched thin, overwhelmed by all the things I said yes to. This has been one of my most vexing lessons—one I struggle with to this day.

When you're discerning, the fleece you gather isn't taken through effort or proof. It's received by noticing what life is offering when you stop chasing.

Fetching the Water of the Styx – Remembering Faith

After we learn to move with the rhythm of life instead of against it, another truth emerges. Even flow has its limits. There comes a moment when clarity and discernment are not enough, when the path asks for something greater than effort, timing, or wisdom. It asks for faith.

Sometimes the tools we once wielded with skill stop working. That's what happened to me.

Somewhere along the line, I learned how to desire a thing so hard that it had to show up. This was especially true with money.

I started my business in 2000 when I was unceremoniously laid off from my job as a proposal writer. I was young and inexperienced, but my expenses were low, so I was able to cobble together enough income to pay my bills.

Over the years, money was a wild ride, but when things got really tough, I could still flex my manifestation muscle, and the right idea would always come.

Fast forward 25 years. I was in much the same place, still scrambling to meet my obligations, still overwhelmed by all my yesses. But now I had a mortgage. And a car payment. And eggs were $8/dozen. I went to the well, flexing that old familiar muscle.

And nothing happened. No brilliant ideas. No new customers out of the blue. No one on the books left to bill. Crickets. The method

I'd used reliably for years to get myself out of a financial jam just stopped working.

When that happens, no amount of planning, strength, or striving will bridge the gap. You have no choice but to learn to trust that your next great chapter is coming.

When the girl within you has tried every way she knows—logic, hustle, charm, perfection—and nothing's worked, the only thing left to do is let go. Not in defeat, but in devotion. When you do, something vast and unseen rushes in to meet you. Help appears from beyond your control, reminding you that you were never meant to carry it all alone.

That's happened to me too.

Remembering the girl in this stage means remembering that surrender is not weakness. It's the doorway through which grace enters. The water you could never reach by force is brought to you when you believe.

Descending to the Underworld – Remembering Wholeness

When we've learned to trust what moves beneath the surface, life leads us one step further, into the place where trust becomes knowing.

Here, even faith falls silent. You've stopped forcing, stopped chasing, even stopped asking. What's left is you, wondering if you've done enough.

Enough. That elusive state of being. When you've pushed hard your entire life, when you've battled your conditioning and your karma, when you've done everything perfectly and your life still doesn't match what you see on your vision board or in magazine ads or on social media, it's easy to think that there's something wrong with you.

The world is telling you that you are not enough. But you *are* enough. You have always been enough. You will always be enough. This is the final illusion to lay down: that worth must be earned.

The girl within you already knows better. She remembers that you were enough before the work began, before the loss and the healing, before the striving to become someone worthy of love.

Even when you forget, she doesn't. She waits in the dark, certain that you will find your way back to your inner knowing.

To remember the girl is to remember yourself—not fixed or flawless, but whole. Not *finally* enough, but *always* enough.

The Writing Life

"Larasa" was not the end of my writing life. Not even close.

After high school, I applied early-decision to McDaniel College, a small liberal arts school in Westminster, Maryland. It was all Georgian-inspired architecture—red brick buildings and stone arches. When I think about those days now, the sky was always blue and the sun was always shining. I loved it there.

The liberal arts education, which ideally consists of four years of academic meandering, is all but lost to us now. College is too expensive to indulge in curiosity. But in those days, you could spend four years earning a degree and still have no idea what you wanted to do with your life.

Or maybe that only applies to English majors.

I emerged from college well-read and totally unskilled in any particular career. Having grown up with two parents who worked in the schools, the only thing I knew for sure was that I didn't want to be a teacher. Fortunately, no one is better at learning how to do things out of books than the venerable English major.

I got a job as a proposal writer, then one in corporate communications for an IT company. After that, I worked as a proposal writer at a construction company.

That was the last "real" job I ever had. And for good reason.

Layoffs were happening across the company, but I thought I was safe. Who fires the person who writes proposals to bring in new business at the moment they most need new business?

Someone who's rich and pretty arrogant, it turns out.

The owner of the company did it himself, after, as I later learned, all five vice presidents joined forces in a valiant campaign to change his mind. (Love those guys, always.)

My big boss called me into his office, which never happened. I sat gingerly on the edge of his guest chair. "We no longer require your services," he said. And that was it.

I went home, cracked open a beer, and told myself I would never put my livelihood in the hands of another person as long as I lived. From there, it played out like a revenge fantasy. The company hired me as a freelancer to write their proposals. I made more from them in that first year than I would have if I'd continued working there as an employee.

One day, as I sat in my old office assembling the required eight copies of my latest 150 page proposal, the owner leaned his head in.

"I'm pretty pleased with myself," he said. "If I hadn't let you go, you wouldn't be where you are now."

Yeah. He really said that.

That deepened my resolve, and a year later, when my existing contacts had run out of work for me, I decided to put my introversion on a shelf and learn how to sell. Because I was never, ever going back.

I spent the next 25 years as a glorified freelancer with a fancy website. I bought books on marketing strategy and color theory. I discovered a love of programming and taught myself how to do that too. It was hard. I made and lost huge sums of money over that time. But I'm so grateful, because that business helped to feed me and my family for a long, long time.

Over the years, I wore out the old excuse that I couldn't write for myself because I wrote marketing copy all day. But I carried a torch for the writing life. I read blog posts like "Morning Routines of 10 Famous Authors" and "8 Ways to Earn Money With Fiction." I read *Bird By Bird* by Anne Lamott, *On Writing* by Stephen King, *War of Art* by Steven Pressfield, and many others. I joined writing groups. I went to conferences. I did everything I could think of to make myself write.

Nothing worked. I just couldn't form the habit.

Then I remembered clarity. I stopped pushing. I accepted that I might never finish a single book. I stood still, patiently waiting to see what happened next.

I remembered timing. I looked at the wreckage of my many abandoned writing projects and refused to start anything new. I resolved to wait for the right opportunity, the book that had to come out of me, no matter what.

I remembered faith. I trusted that everything would unfold in right timing. I stopped putting pressure on myself and started watching for the nudges that would send me in the right direction.

I remembered wholeness. I dropped the idea that my writing wasn't good enough, or nobody would like it. I decided I was worthy of expressing my truth, whether anybody noticed or not.

I remembered the girl. The sweet silence of getting lost in a novel, like the ones I'd loved in school. *David Copperfield. The Sound and the Fury. The Adventures of Huckleberry Finn.*

Like Psyche opening her eyes to Eros, I saw that the writing life had never really left me. It had only been waiting for me to come home.

Maybe you don't remember a time when you weren't striving. Maybe you learned too early that love and approval were things you had to earn. That being capable and productive were the only ways to stay safe.

But somewhere, beneath all that effort, the girl within you remembers. Not in memories or words, but in the quiet hum that rises when you're completely absorbed in something real—like a little girl bent over her coloring, unaware of who's watching or what comes next. That hum has never left you. It's the sound of being whole.

Midlife invites you back to that place. After years of proving yourself to parents, bosses, partners, and even yourself, you begin to realize you no longer have to keep auditioning for your life. You know what you know. You've built a body of work and a body of wisdom. You can stand in both without apology.

This is what remembering the girl feels like now: not fragile or naïve, but steady. You don't need to perform your worth or chase belonging. You can simply meet the world with the quiet confidence that says, *Here I am.*

And when you live from that hum, when your worth and your work flow from the same still place, you begin to understand that you were never becoming enough. You were enough all along.

Gentle Calls to Action

When you reach this point in the journey, knowing you are enough isn't just an idea—it's something you begin to live. It shows up in the small ways as you move through your days, in the moments when you choose trust over tension, rest over striving, presence over performance. These are not grand gestures, but quiet acts of remembering.

When something in your life isn't working, notice your instinct to push harder. Instead, pause. Step back. Ask yourself gently, "What's mine to carry, and what can I set down?" Sometimes clarity arrives not through effort, but through stillness.

Pay attention to your timing. The world moves in rhythms, and not every door opens at once. You don't have to rush toward what isn't ready. Wait for the heat of the day to pass. Trust that what's meant for you will be there when the time is right.

Let yourself be helped. When a hand reaches out—a neighbor's kindness, a colleague's insight, a friend's quiet support—practice saying yes. Receiving is its own form of courage.

Notice when you are performing. In those moments, breathe and remind yourself: *I know what I know. Here I am.* You don't have to convince anyone of your worth.

Then, whenever you can, follow the hum. Do something simply because it brings you peace or joy. Let yourself be absorbed in it—like the little girl coloring, lost in her own world. That hum is the truest sound of coming home.

This is the practice of remembering the girl—not something you think about, but something you live into, again and again. Every pause, every breath, every act of trust brings you a little closer to her. And one day, without even realizing it, you'll find that the hum is no longer something you have to return to. It's simply who you are.

Ritual Suggestion

Sometimes it helps to give remembering a shape, something your hands can touch. You might create a small ritual to remind yourself that worthiness doesn't need to be earned. Find a quiet space and gather a few things: a bowl, a candle, and a few things to hold your intentions—seeds, stones, or anything small enough to rest in your palm.

Light the candle and take a few deep breaths. Let your body settle. Pick up the seed or stone and think of something you've been trying to prove: that you're competent, lovable, relevant, strong enough, young enough, still needed. Name it quietly, and then let it go. Place it in the bowl. Continue until you've said everything that wants to be released. Feel the weight of the bowl in your hands, heavy with all the striving you no longer need to carry.

Whisper, "I release what I no longer have to earn." Sit for a moment in the silence that follows. Notice the ease that begins to rise in the space you've cleared.

When you're ready, take the bowl outside. Pour the contents into the earth, returning what was never yours to hold. Leave the bowl empty on your table for a while—a reminder that you don't have to fill every space. Sometimes emptiness is its own form of grace.

Journal Prompts

As always, let these questions meet you where you are—not as assignments to complete, but as gentle doorways back to yourself.

Remembering Clarity

- Where in my life am I trying to sort what's truly mine to carry from what belongs to someone else?
- What happens when I stop pushing and let clarity come to me instead of chasing it?

Remembering Timing

- What have I learned about my own timing—the moments when it's better to wait, listen, or rest?

- Where might "being brave" actually mean holding back and trusting that life will move when it's ready?

Remembering Faith

- When have I reached my limits and discovered that help appeared only after I stopped trying to do it all myself?
- What would it feel like to let myself be supported — by people, by spirit, by something larger than my own effort?

Remembering Wholeness

- What do I still believe I need to prove to be worthy of love, respect, or success?
- If I stopped striving for a moment, what quiet truth might I hear about who I already am?

Remembering the Girl

- When do I feel that quiet hum—the feeling of being absorbed in something that feels like me?
- How might I bring that same presence into my work, relationships, or daily rhythm?

The Girl You Once Were

The girl you once were never disappeared. She's been waiting in the quiet spaces, between and beyond all your doing. She doesn't need you to return to childhood, only to remember what it felt like to be alive without performance or permission.

As you reach back for her, notice what stirs inside you. Is it her laughter, her wonder, her unguarded heart? These are not relics of who you used to be, but the roots of who you still are. Let them soften you. Let them remind you that joy was once simple, and that stillness was once safe.

Chapter 5

Claiming the Quiet

I've never felt like I was part of a group.

It started on the first day of first grade. At the beginning of recess, a group of kids were standing by the monkey bars. The leader said, "Okay, let's go around and say how old you are."

Six. Six. Six. Six. Six.

Then it came to me.

"I'm five," I said.

"Five!" the leader exclaimed. "How can you be five?"

"My birthday is in November."

It seemed reasonable to me. If you turned six before the end of the calendar year, you could start first grade. My mother was eager to get me out of her hair and, to be fair, there was no reason to hold me back.

"No five year olds," the leader said. "You can't play with us. Go away."

That's the first time I remember feeling so roundly rejected over something I couldn't control. It wasn't the last.

It was easy enough to pretend that everything was okay when I was in class. I was smart, so my teachers liked me. But lunchtime was another matter. All those kids, interacting with one another freely, judging each other based on what clothes they wore, what was on their lunchbox, and whether they had any good food to trade.

I did not do well in that situation.

Every fall, for the first few weeks of school, I'd try to fit in. But so did everybody else. And it didn't take long for the weirdos to get pushed out.

Sixth grade was a tough one. There were two tables assigned to our class—long tables with benches on each side—and for some reason, our little hive mind decided you just *had* to be at Table A. So we all crawled over each other trying to squeeze in, while Table B sat empty.

Eventually the social order ejected me. I remember thinking of it as my own choice. "This is stupid," I said to myself. "I'm just going to sit over here by myself."

The next day, another weirdo from my class came over. "Can I sit here?" she asked. I nodded. She placed her tray down across from me and climbed onto the bench.

"It's stupid," she said, "trying to squeeze in over there."

Finally, someone who made sense.

That girl's name was Alison, and she was the first best friend I ever had.

When you're different, sometimes your best play is to fade into the background so no one notices you. If they don't notice you, they can't call you names. When you spend a lot of time alone like I did, you're everywhere and nowhere. Just like Hestia.

Meet Hestia

When the world was new, there were six children born to the Titans Kronos and Rhea: Hestia, Demeter, Hera, Hades, Poseidon, and Zeus. Kronos knew of the prophecy—one of them would rise up and destroy him. So he did what any sensible father would do. He devoured each child as soon as they were born.

(Listen, I told you I don't make the myths.)

Anyway, Hestia was the eldest and the first to be swallowed.

Alone inside her father's belly, Hestia learned patience. She learned how to breathe in darkness. How to keep a spark alive when everything around her was swallowed in shadow.

Years passed and, one by one, her siblings joined her. Then Zeus, the youngest, was born. Their mother, Rhea, hid him away and tricked Kronos into swallowing a swaddled stone in his place. When Zeus grew to manhood, he forced Kronos to regurgitate his siblings and led them in rebellion against the Titans. Together they built a new order, each claiming a dominion of the world their parents had ruled.

Zeus took the sky. Poseidon claimed the sea. Hades descended into the underworld. Hera became goddess of marriage and sovereignty. Demeter made the fields bloom with grain and fruit.

And then there was Hestia.

She stood apart as her siblings divided creation among themselves. She had been the first to enter the darkness and the last to emerge from it. She knew the weight of hunger and the taste of silence. She wanted no throne, no dominion. When Zeus asked what she desired, she answered quietly:

Let me live in the heart of every home. Let me be the fire that warms and the light that guides. Let me be peace itself.

It was such a simple request that Zeus agreed without hesitation. And so Hestia took her place—not on Olympus, but at the hearth of every dwelling, in the coals that glowed through the night and the smoke that curled toward the stars.

Wherever a flame was kindled, she was there. When a traveler crossed a threshold and whispered thanks for warmth, it was to her. When bread was shared, the first crumb was given to her fire. Hestia was the unseen thread that bound the living to their ancestors, the hearth to the home, and the home to the world beyond.

In every city, her flame burned in the public hall—the Prytaneion—where citizens gathered to settle disputes, welcome strangers, and celebrate peace. When colonies were founded, settlers carried embers from that sacred fire to light the first hearth in the new land, a promise that, even far from home, they were still connected.

Hestia's story is quiet. She fought no wars, sent forth no heroes, stirred no jealousies among the gods. While others battled for dominion, she simply tended her flame. Poseidon offered her the treasures of the deep. Apollo wooed her with songs of gold and prophecy. But Hestia refused them both. She laid her hand upon Zeus's head and swore an oath by the river Styx to remain whole unto herself—unclaimed, undivided, untouched.

This was not a rejection of love, but a deeper kind of devotion. She would belong to everyone by belonging first to herself.

While the heavens thundered and the sea raged, Hestia sat still at the center of things. She was the pause before prayer, the stillness after song, the light that endured when the world grew dark. Her power was presence. Her reign was peace.

In the great myths of gods and mortals, her name is rarely shouted. Poets did not sing of her because her story held no spectacle. Yet every offering began and ended with her. Without her flame, no sacrifice reached the gods. Without her, no home could hold.

Hestia's gift was not noise or conquest, but constancy. The quiet she claimed was not emptiness—it was fullness, a wholeness born of choosing to be where she was.

In a world that prizes the loud and the visible, her example remains radical. She reminds us that there is sacredness in tending what endures: the daily rituals, the small acts of care, the moments of stillness that keep the world from burning itself to ash.

Hestia teaches that peace is not the absence of fire but the tending of it. Her flame still burns—steady and patient, in every kitchen candle and every lamp lit against the dark. After all this time, she whispers the same invitation:

Come home. Be still. Claim the quiet that is already yours.

Belonging To Yourself

Hestia's gift was not power or glory. It was the peace that comes from knowing who you are and where you belong. While her brothers and sisters reached outward, building kingdoms, stirring storms, and ruling life and death, Hestia turned inward. She did not need to be seen to know her worth.

There's something quietly revolutionary about that.

Most of us are taught that belonging is something we earn through approval, success, or usefulness. We look to others to confirm that we're enough. But Hestia reminds us that true belonging begins at home, within our own hearts. Her hearth-fire was never about walls or family names or city gates. It was the living warmth of self-connection, tended day after day, no matter what storms raged outside.

When she refused the hands of Poseidon and Apollo, Hestia wasn't rejecting love. She was honoring the sacred truth that she could not give what she had not first claimed. She belonged to herself before she belonged to anyone else.

This is the essence of coming home.

To belong to yourself is to become the hearth you return to. It means tending the flame of your own aliveness—not waiting for permission, not dimming your light to make others comfortable. It means knowing that quiet is not absence, and stillness is not weakness. It's the place where your soul gathers strength.

Hestia's story calls us to reclaim that quiet center. To resist the pull of noise and comparison. To remember that we don't have to chase worthiness; we can tend it gently, right where we are.

Each time you pause to breathe and listen for what's true, you are tending your own hearth. You are becoming your own sanctuary.

And when you live from that place, you don't have to seek belonging anymore. You are belonging.

Moving to Table B

Belonging to yourself is the missing piece, and it often falls into place at midlife. At this point, many of us have grown tired of comparing ourselves to others and contorting into unnatural shapes just to fit in. This is the time of life when more and more of us realize that we can just move to Table B, and that's where our people will find us.

Here's the thing: Table B is where quiet lives. There, you can be free from all the drama of your busy workplace, the noise of social media buzzing your phone all day and all night, the malaise of believing you are not enough.

It's not comfortable at first. But it's necessary.

I stumbled into this early when Mr. Moneybags fired me from my dead end proposal writing job. I told myself that owning my own business would free me from the existential dread of losing another job, and it did. But it also freed me from working in an office, which inevitably comes with drama and politics.

This was not the age of telework. Plenty of people thought that striking out on my own was too risky. That I would come to my senses soon enough and start scouring the newspaper for help wanted ads. I named my company Bevans Group and talked about "my team" in every pitch, because in those days, nobody would hire a lone wolf to design their brand or their website, let alone a woman.

Am I being too dramatic? Ask the lady who heard my business name and immediately asked, "How do you like working with your husband?" Yeah. She really said that.

Two separate times, when things got tight, I took part time contract positions to make ends meet. Those positions required me to commute over an hour each way, three days a week. I took the first one just before I got pregnant. I told them I would stay until my son was born, but I didn't last that long. The day my boss walked into my office and told me I needed to wear better shoes, I started looking for the exit ramp.

The second contract position came along just after I separated from Dave. Even though I'd been planning to leave for a while, to be honest, I wasn't financially prepared to move out of the house and support myself. (Impulsive, remember?) I called my friend Karen and asked if she could use me a few days a week. I am eternally grateful she said yes, and I'm happy to say I've made significant contributions to her team since then.

The downside? I had to go into the office. Commuting. Chatter around the coffee maker. Real pants. I love her team, but that was never for me. So when COVID-19 hit and we all went home, I was relieved.

We all learned a lot about the quiet in those days. When every trip to the grocery store was potentially deadly, staying home just felt like a better idea. Families and organizations everywhere had to figure out how to navigate working from home, remote school, vaccine distribution—all of it.

But we also learned to bake sourdough. We organized our cupboards and pulled out the board games. We took walks around the neighborhood. We transferred those hours we used to spend commuting to meaning-making activities, time with our families, time for ourselves. And employers adjusted. At least for a little while.

Don't get me wrong. A lot of people suffered terribly during the pandemic, trying in vain to make ends meet. Small businesses were hit especially hard. But I, and many women I know, thrived. We stretched ourselves wide and took up every bit of space that pandemic living allowed us. Some of us found it impossible to go back to the way things were before.

That's the power and the beauty of Table B. When you stop trying to squeeze in, stop trying to prove that you're worthy of a tiny sliver of space, the whole world opens up to you. You can begin to ask yourself questions like, *Why am I here? What am I meant to do? What is it all for?*

But first, you need to make space. This is what claiming the quiet can do.

Your People Find You

Moving to Table B opens up new possibilities. In a way, I moved to Table B when I moved out of the house and into my own place. And almost immediately, my person found me.

John and I had been Facebook friends for 10 years. I forget who friended who. It was just one of those "oh look, we have friends in common" deals. I didn't think anything of it, and neither did he. We would just wish each other a happy birthday and occasionally like each other's posts when they came across our respective feeds.

But at some point, I found myself lingering a little longer on those posts. Something was stirring.

One day, I noticed that John and another friend had both indicated interest in an upcoming crab feast. The event was very close to my house—just the next town over. By that point, Dave and I were already living separate lives. Almost everything I did, I did on my own. So I took a chance and messaged them both:

"Are either of you actually planning to go to this? I'm tired of going to these things by myself."

They both said yes.

The day of the crab feast arrived. As John tells it, he noticed me coming as I crossed the parking lot and skipped down the few steps to the patio. His first thought was, "Wow. She's tall."

We sat next to each other and picked crabs. I thought it was funny that he was wearing latex gloves. He insisted that he had a cut on his finger and that's why (Old Bay stings). By the end of the night, we were hunkered down under a patio umbrella, waiting out a surprise thunderstorm.

Looking back, it's easy to see that, as we pressed ourselves together, trying in vain to stay dry, we were already in love.

A few weeks later, I moved into my apartment, and John and I started dating. I wasn't looking for a relationship that soon. I wanted to be free. But there was no denying that our love was powerful.

When we rest in the quiet, our intuition comes alive. It's easier to detect who's right for us and who isn't. That's one of the most powerful lessons of the initiation—that when we create stillness, we can finally know who we are. Not in comparison to others, but on our own. And when we know who we are, we know what to do. Every time.

In every season of life, the quiet takes a new form. Sometimes it looks like solitude. Sometimes it looks like love that doesn't demand performance. And sometimes it looks like learning, at last, to rest inside yourself.

Claiming the Quiet in the Midst of a Busy Life

In a noisy world, quiet rarely arrives on its own. It must be claimed, tended like a small, stubborn flame. Hestia knew this. While her brothers and sisters divided the heavens, the seas, and the underworld, she chose no kingdom at all. She claimed the hearth. She made peace her dominion.

Every home had its fire, and every fire belonged to her. Yet her power was never about control. It was about presence. She didn't chase glory or demand attention. She simply kept the flame alive. And because she did, life itself could continue. Meals were cooked. Families gathered. Travelers found warmth. Civilization endured because one goddess chose to be still.

That is what it means to claim the quiet. To stand, as Hestia did, in the center of your own life and say, "This space is sacred. This is where the fire lives."

We all have a hearth inside of us. It's easy to forget it exists when the world pulls us outward with endless demands. The phone buzzes, the inbox fills, the to-do list lengthens, and somewhere in the noise, we lose the plot of our own lives. But the hearth doesn't go out. The embers remain, glowing softly, waiting for us to breathe into them by claiming the quiet.

You don't have to retreat to a monastery or escape your responsibilities. Hestia's temple was never a fortress apart from the world; it was woven into its very center. Every home, every city, every gathering place held her fire. That's our invitation—to carry the hearth with us into ordinary life.

You can begin with a single breath. Let it draw you back from the swirl of tasks and expectations. Feel your feet on the floor, the air in your lungs, the pulse in your hands. Imagine a small, steady flame at your center. Neither raging nor dying, simply alive. That is Hestia's fire in you.

When you tend that flame, you begin to notice how much of your busyness is performance. The world teaches that constant motion proves how important you are, but Hestia reminds us that constancy is deeper than motion. The hearth won't chase you. It waits silently for your return.

Claiming the quiet means daring to stop, even briefly, and trust that your value doesn't vanish when you do. It means giving yourself permission to be enough as you are, right now, in this breath. It means saying no when the fire needs tending, not because you don't care, but because you do.

As you practice, quiet begins to move with you. It's there in the way you stir your coffee, fold the laundry, close your laptop. The hearth becomes portable. The flame goes wherever you go.

Hestia's lesson is timeless: peace is not passive. It's an act of devotion. Every time you choose stillness over striving, you're not retreating from the world, you're keeping it alive. The fire doesn't burn without a keeper.

Be that keeper. Claim your quiet. Let your life be the hearth that warms everything you touch.

Gentle Calls to Action

Begin by noticing the flame within you. You don't have to build a raging bonfire. The embers are already there, glowing quietly beneath the noise of the day. Pause long enough to feel their warmth. Place a hand on your heart. Breathe deeply and imagine that each breath fans the coals of your own peace.

Let yourself move a little slower. Make a cup of tea and drink it without multitasking. Sit beside a candle and gaze into the flickering flame. Choose one small ritual that brings you back to yourself—lighting a fire, tending a plant, feeding your pets, journaling before bed—and treat it as holy. These are not small things. They are how we remember who we are.

When the world demands more than you can give, when others pull at your energy and attention, return to your hearth. Ask yourself,

What do I need right now to feel at home in my body? Then honor the answer, even if it means saying no. Especially if it means saying no.

You don't have to earn rest. You don't have to prove your value through motion. Hestia's lesson is that presence is enough. The fire burns brightest, not when it's fanned wildly, but when it's tended with care.

So tend yourself. Be the keeper of your own warmth. Let your quiet become your strength, your belonging, and your offering to the world.

Ritual Suggestion

This ritual can be practiced whenever you feel scattered, depleted, or unsure where you stand. It's a gentle way to return to your center, to remember that home is not something you must find, but something you can reclaim.

Begin by finding a quiet space. It doesn't have to be perfect—just a small, comfortable place where you can breathe. Bring with you a candle or a small light source and something that feels like home to you: a photograph, a smooth stone, a favorite mug, a key, or a piece of fabric worn soft by time.

Place the object before you and light the candle. Watch the flame for a few moments. Let it flicker and dance without trying to shape it. This is your inner fire—steady, alive, and entirely yours.

As you breathe, imagine this flame living within your chest. Feel its warmth spreading down your arms and into your hands, through your belly and hips, into your legs and down to the soles of your feet. With every breath, feel yourself coming home to your own presence.

When you are ready, whisper softly: "I belong to myself. I am safe in my own presence. I carry my fire wherever I go." Let the words linger. Close your eyes if you wish, and notice what belonging feels like inside your body.

When you feel complete, blow out the candle or turn off the light. Imagine that the flame remains inside you, burning quietly, a constant companion to guide you back whenever you drift too far from yourself. Sit for a few moments longer, allowing the stillness to settle around you.

You might take a few minutes to write or simply reflect. Ask yourself, what helps me feel at home in myself? Where have I been giving my energy away? How can I best tend my inner flame? There are no right or wrong answers, only the gentle truth that rises when you give it space to speak.

Carry that truth with you into the day. Let it warm the parts of you that have grown cold from overgiving or striving. Remember, you don't have to chase belonging. You already belong to yourself.

Journal Prompts

- What does belonging to myself mean to me right now? How does it feel in my body when I imagine it?
- Where in my life do I most often give away my peace or power in order to belong to others?
- What are the small, ordinary things that make me feel most at home in myself?
- When I am quiet, what do I notice about who I am and what I need?
- What would it look like to tend my inner hearth with the same care I give to others?

- How can I create a daily ritual that reminds me I am my own safe place?

- In what ways have I mistaken motion for meaning, or noise for worth? What would it look like to choose stillness instead?

- How can I honor the ebbs and flows of my energy without apology?

- What helps me remember that I am the flame, not just the keeper of it?

Coming Home to the Quiet

To belong to yourself is to remember that your worth does not depend on how brightly you shine, but on how faithfully you tend your light. Hestia teaches us that peace is not the absence of fire—it is the steadiness of a constant flame. When we choose quiet over chaos, presence over performance, we begin to feel the ground beneath our own feet again. We stop reaching outward for affirmation and start listening inward for truth.

This is the work of claiming the quiet: learning to trust that stillness is not emptiness, but fertile ground. It is here, in the calm center of your own being, that something ancient begins to stir. When you no longer chase belonging, you create space for something softer to rise—something that feels like grace, like breath, like the first spark of wonder returning to your hands.

Chapter 6
Inviting Magic Back In

Dad had been ready to go for a while.

After Mom died, he lived in the house for a few months, but the loneliness was too much for him. So he gave away his dog, sold the house my sister and I grew up in, and moved to a senior living community.

Before long, he fell in with a group of friends. They had dinner together every night, and I got to know them pretty well over the years. Every once in a while, a friend would miss a night, then two. Someone would check on them and report back. "Oh, she's not feeling well. She'll be back in a few days." Sometimes they never came back, and it turned out they had moved to assisted living or nursing care or had died. Eventually another resident would join the group.

Dad lived there for nine years. His mobility and cognition declined—slowly at first, then suddenly and catastrophically, exacerbated by his isolation during the pandemic, when the dining room was closed to residents and the entire campus was closed to visitors for months on end.

One Tuesday in August 2022, I got a call from a paramedic. Dad had fallen in his bathroom in the middle of the night.

"Can you tell me how your dad is mentally most of the time? Does he usually know what's going on?"

"Yeah, he's pretty sharp. Why?"

"Well, he's not making a whole lot of sense right now."

That was Dad's first episode of delirium.

Things spiraled after that, and it didn't take long before he was in nursing care. The idea of continuing care had been reassuring on paper, but once it happened, none of us were happy, least of all Dad. His cognition was failing, and he was embarrassed that he couldn't remember things, so he stayed in his room most of the time, even though he could have gone to the dining room for meals. Eventually, he was confined to a wheelchair and spent his days watching old game shows on television.

One day, while I was visiting, he became agitated. "I don't understand, Annie. Why am I still here?"

He looked at the photo of my mother, which we had placed on the windowsill.

His voice breaking, he said, "I hardly remember her." Then he looked at me, eyes shining, and asked, "Why am I here? I just want to go and be with my dad."

Two weeks later, he stopped getting out of bed. He could no longer tell the difference between things that happened in real life and things that happened in dreams. One day, he told me that he had been walking across the dining room and someone had tripped him. I didn't remind him he hadn't walked anywhere in weeks. I just rolled with it.

Another day he told me that someone had come from his church to give him communion. Although dad was a lifelong Christian and had given so much, in terms of time, talent and money, to his church, I hadn't heard of anyone coming to see him ever, so I thought he had imagined it. I let that daydream lie too, realizing it was giving him comfort.

A few days later he died.

After his funeral, a man came up to me. "I wanted to tell you, I saw your dad just a few days ago. I gave him communion."

I was flabbergasted. I was so sure Dad had imagined it, yet the man was standing right in front of me.

"I couldn't find him at first," he continued. "I guess he had moved." That was true. He had moved to a different room a couple of weeks before he died. "But something told me I had to see him that day, so I went down to the front desk to ask. It took them quite a while to figure out where he was."

Of course. My dad, who had believed so strongly in God and country, who had played music and led choirs in churches since he was 16 years old, was waiting to receive communion one last time. And he didn't even know it.

This man could have given up when Dad wasn't where he was supposed to be, but he didn't. He found him, and he gave him what he needed.

To me, this is the magic of being alive. These are the miracles that shape our lives. And they will keep happening, even if you don't notice them. Even when you're 87 and all you want to do is go home.

Meet Brigid

In Irish mythology, there was a goddess who belonged to both hearth and sky. Her name was Brigid. She was a daughter of the Dagda and was beloved by poets and midwives, smiths and healers.

Brigid was born at the break of dawn, when the first light touched the earth and the world held its breath between night and day. From the moment she opened her eyes, she carried three gifts that would never fade: the flame of inspiration, the healing of the waters, and the strength of the forge.

Brigid's flame stirred poets and musicians to sing what could not otherwise be spoken. Her waters brought comfort to the weary and mended what was broken, whether in body or spirit. And at her forge, she shaped not only metal, but destiny itself, tempering it with fire and grace.

Wherever Brigid walked, blessings followed. Fields ripened. Wells overflowed. Cows gave milk so rich it shone like gold in the sun. The people felt her in their bones and breath, in the rhythm of their work and the warmth of their homes. They called upon her at birth and at death, in joy and in sorrow, for she was a goddess who understood both.

When her son was slain in battle, Brigid wept. Her cry was the first keening, a song of grief so fierce it split the sky. From that moment, women have wailed at gravesides not to despair, but to honor the love that no longer had a place to go. Brigid taught them that grief itself is holy—that heartbreak is part of becoming.

Her flame was tended for centuries in Kildare, kept alive by nineteen women who guarded it night and day. On the twentieth night, it was said, the goddess herself would come to watch. Even when the old gods were plastered over by invading armies and missionaries, Brigid remained. The people remembered her as Saint Brigid, Abbess of Kildare, and her flame still burned—first in a temple, then in a convent, and finally in the hearts of those who refused to forget.

At Imbolc, when winter loosens its grip and lambs are born, her spirit walks the land once more. Households leave a door unlatched for her, cloths on the sill to catch her blessing. By morning, frost has softened, and snowdrops bloom where her feet have passed. The people say she travels with white cows whose breath turns ice to flowers.

Brigid is not a goddess of thunder or conquest. She is a goddess of the threshold—the one who waits between night and morning, winter and spring, sorrow and renewal. Her magic is not distant or dramatic; it is woven into daily life. The rising loaf. The healing cup of tea. The warmth of a hand held through grief.

To light a candle, to pour clear water, to shape something beautiful or useful with your own two hands. These, too, are acts of Brigid. She reminds us that magic was never meant to be rare. It was meant to live among us.

Her story endures because she does not ask us to leave the world to find the sacred. She asks us to notice it where we already are. To tend our inner flame, to keep it burning even when the wind howls. She invites us to remember that creativity, compassion, and courage are all forms of fire. And that when we tend them, we invite the magic back in.

Everyday Magic

Brigid's story reminds us that magic has never really left us—it's just been waiting for us to notice it again. We think of magic as something grand or otherworldly, but Brigid teaches that it lives in the ordinary. The same fire that glows on her altar burns in our kitchen stoves and candles. The same water that fills her wells flows from our taps and falls as rain. The same spark that guided her hand at the forge flickers in us when we create, comfort, and care.

Inviting magic back into your life doesn't require rituals or rare ingredients. It asks only that you soften your gaze and pay attention. When you stir a pot of soup with love, you are practicing kitchen magic. When you write a poem, plant a seed, or mend a torn sleeve, you are shaping the world with intention. When you speak gently to yourself after a long day, you are tending your inner flame.

Brigid's presence lingers wherever something is made, healed, or transformed. Her gift is not to give you power, but to remind you that you already have it—that the divine is not separate from your daily life, but woven through it.

When you sweep your hearth, light a candle, or whisper a prayer for the coming day, you echo the old traditions that kept her flame alive. You become the twentieth woman at Kildare, keeping watch as the goddess rests.

Inviting the magic back in is not about escape, it's about returning to the rhythm of your breath, the warmth of your body, the pulse of life that moves through all things. It's about remembering that the sacred was never lost; it was only waiting for you to look up from the noise and see it again.

Expect Miracles

When John and I first got together, back when I'd scrawled *expect miracles* on my refrigerator, I had no idea what twists and turns awaited us.

My son's father, Dave, had very good insurance through his work, and early in our separation, he suggested that we hold off on divorcing so I could continue to enjoy those benefits. I was so grateful, since health insurance is expensive and I was pretty broke.

But negotiating the separation agreement was difficult, and the day after it was signed, my lawyer called to tell me that Dave had filed for divorce.

Even after everything that had happened, I was surprised and hurt. I was working at Karen's company part time, but she didn't offer health insurance, and I wasn't really in a position to buy it for myself.

Still, with my health history, it would have been unwise not to have health insurance. So I did what I had to do. I got the money together and signed up for an HMO.

As I was filling out the paperwork, something told me that I should add John to my policy. We hadn't been together very long, but the feeling wouldn't go away, so even though it seemed like it was too soon, I insured him as well.

Shortly after that, John started having a lot of trouble with his hip. It got so bad, he started walking with a cane. He visited a chiropractor and tried acupuncture, but it only seemed to be getting worse. Fortunately, because of my impulsive decision (or inner knowing—you be the judge) to add him to my insurance, he had access to the healthcare he needed. And what he needed was a hip replacement.

We navigated the long process of pre-surgical testing, only to learn that a blood marker that indicated a risk of clots was very high. John's dad had circulatory problems, so we naturally thought that was the issue. But the levels didn't come down, even after months on heavy doses of blood thinners.

During one visit, our doctor tilted her head to one side, thinking. "John, we've scanned every part of your body except your belly. I'm going to order a CT scan."

On some level, she already knew, just like my doctor knew years earlier when she squeezed blood out of my nipple.

A week later, we learned that John had kidney cancer.

Looking back at photos from just before his diagnosis, it's a wonder we didn't realize something was wrong. In one photo, he's standing next to our cargo trailer, leaning on his cane, with an enormous belly. He thought he had just gained weight, and I hadn't thought about it at all.

The only way to treat John's type of cancer was surgery. So a week after his diagnosis, he walked back into pre-op and I set up in the waiting room with my laptop and an entire package of Oreos. (That's how I cope, okay?)

The surgery went well, and after a few months of recovery, John had his hip replacement as well.

It isn't lost on me. If Dave and I had followed through on his plan to stay married a little longer, I wouldn't have bought health insurance for myself. And if I hadn't bought health insurance for myself, I wouldn't have bought health insurance for John. And if John didn't have health insurance, he wouldn't have gone to the doctor about his hip. And if he hadn't gone to the doctor about his hip, we wouldn't have discovered his cancer until it was too late.

And that's the story of how my ex-husband, and a healthy dose of everyday magic, saved my great love's life.

Numbers On Fire

The magic you're inviting back in is capable of more than orchestrating events in your everyday life. It can help you see beyond this world to what lies beneath.

Before I married Dave, I married my college sweetheart. If there's anything Chris and I would agree on, it's that our marriage was a painful, drawn-out affair that left both of us better off the moment the divorce papers were signed.

The worst part, by far, of ending my first marriage was losing contact with my former in-laws, especially my mother-in-law, Sandee, and her mother, whom we called J.

J and I were fast friends. I spent hours sitting under the gold crucifix that hung over her proper, floral sofa, listening to her stories. I especially liked the one where the iceman came, hauling enormous blocks of ice with giant metal tongs.

"We didn't have a refrigerator," J would tell me, wide-eyed, as if she scarcely believed it herself. "No one did. We had an icebox, and every day the iceman would come with a fresh delivery."

Occasionally, I would take J to the grocery store. "Get a buggy," she'd call as we crossed the parking lot. J was the only person I knew who called a shopping cart a buggy, and I instantly adopted the practice.

There were many moments, both during my ill-fated marriage and after, that I considered the possibility that J liked me better than she liked her own grandson.

Years later, I found myself pulling into a rest stop along I-95, barely awake, hands clutching the steering wheel at 10 and 2. Samson was passed out in the back seat, still in diapers, and Dave was similarly groggy.

Like parents of sleeping toddlers everywhere, we tacitly agreed to take turns in the restroom. Since Dave was barely conscious, I went first. As I crossed the crowded rest-stop toward the ladies' room, I was overtaken by a thought that was not my own:

You should call Sandee.

I paused, just for a moment, then kept walking. After three more paces:

You should call Sandee. Tell her about the cancer. She would want to pray for you.

The second time, the thought was so strong and so obviously foreign that it stopped me in my tracks. She'd want to pray for me? I couldn't remember thinking anything like that...ever.

Once again, I dismissed it. I finished my business and went back to the car. As I got in, Dave heaved himself out of the Corolla and lumbered in the direction of the men's room.

For the third time, someone else's thought hijacked my brain:

You need to call Sandee right now.

"But I haven't talked to her in years," I protested aloud. "I don't even remember her phone number!"

And that's when things got really weird, because there was Sandee's home number, floating in my mind's eye like the burning bush at the top of Mount Sinai. I immediately recognized it and reached for my phone.

"Um, hi Sandee," I began. "I know it's been ages, and this is probably the weirdest voicemail you'll ever receive, but I just got this really strong feeling that I needed to call you. I hope you're okay. Call me back if you want to. If you don't, that's okay too."

When Dave got back to the car, I told him about my strange experience. He shrugged and went back to sleep.

A few hours later, I noticed I had a voicemail:

"Hi Ann. It's Sandee. I can't believe you called me today. I wasn't at home because...well, J passed away today. Could you please call me back?"

It turns out that J had been in hospice for some time. And everyone who needed to had come to say goodbye. Sandee recited the whole list–aunts and uncles and cousins so far removed from my life that I barely remembered them.

That very morning, Sandee had leaned over her mother, who was no longer conscious, and whispered, "Mom, I want you to know that it's okay to go if you're ready. But when you get to wherever you're going, if you can, would you please send me a sign to let me know you're okay?"

A few breaths later, J died.

She found me walking through a crowded rest stop along I-95, looking for the ladies' room.

There are things about this life that we cannot explain. They exist only in our peripheral vision. Turn your head and they'll disappear.

J was as Catholic as they come. She lived and died believing in Jesus and the saints. She prayed to the Virgin Mary. She prayed for me.

I don't know if God gave J a chance to visit me on her way to heaven because she was such a good believer. But I do know this: if there is one person on earth who could make me stop what I was doing, pick up my phone and call my ex-mother-in-law, it was her. And she knew that, if I made the call, Sandee would get the message.

The Magic That Finds You

When you begin to notice the shimmer of the sacred in your everyday life, the world changes shape around you. It's not that miracles suddenly start happening—it's that you finally see the ones that were happening all along. A stranger shows up at exactly the right moment. A doctor trusts her intuition. A thought that isn't quite yours insists on being heard. These are Brigid's fingerprints—the flicker of her flame, the breath that stirs the still air.

Magic is not a trick or a test. It's a conversation. You take one step toward it, and it steps toward you. You set a place at your table, and it arrives in its own time, wearing an ordinary face. The more you practice noticing, the more you are noticed in return.

Brigid's gift is not to rescue us from our humanity, but to illuminate it. She teaches us that even the most mundane acts—washing dishes, making tea, calling an old friend—can become portals when done with presence and love. She reminds us that connection itself is holy.

This is how we invite magic back in: by choosing to believe that life is still capable of surprising us, that the veil between worlds has always been thin, and that every act of care is a small flame in the dark, one the goddess just might see and smile upon.

Gentle Calls to Action

Begin by softening your gaze. Look around the space you inhabit right now—the light coming through the window, the warmth of your coffee cup, the hum of something alive and ordinary. Let yourself remember that this, too, is sacred. You don't have to earn magic or chase it down. You only have to notice it.

Light a candle when you start your day, not to invoke anything grand, but to honor your own flame. Watch how it wavers, but it continues to burn. Let it remind you that you are still here, still becoming, still part of the great rhythm that turns night into morning.

Make soup. Stir it slowly. Offer gratitude for the ingredients, for the hands that grew and gathered them, and for the nourishment they'll bring. Every act of creation, no matter how small, is an invitation for life to meet you halfway.

Let your work, your craft, or your care for others become a kind of prayer. When you write a line that feels true, when you mend something broken, when you reach out to someone who's lonely, imagine Brigid's presence beside you—steady, luminous, and kind. These moments are how we keep the flame alive.

And at the end of the day, before you turn out the lights, whisper a quiet thank-you for what you can't explain—the perfect timing, the invisible hand, the way love still finds you through the cracks. The world is always speaking to you in its own language of wonder. All you have to do is listen.

Ritual Suggestion

Choose one small act in your daily life and turn it into a blessing. It could be lighting a candle, brewing your morning tea, feeding your pets, or washing the dishes after dinner. Something so familiar that you usually move through it without a thought.

Before you begin, pause for just a moment. Take a breath and notice the weight of your body, the air in the room, the sound of your own heartbeat. Whisper a quiet invocation, if it feels right: "May this simple act become sacred. May I remember that life itself is holy."

Then, as you move through the task, bring your full attention to it. Let the warmth of the water, the scent of the soap, or the rhythm of your movements become a kind of prayer. Imagine that Brigid's flame is near you, steady and watchful, illuminating this ordinary moment.

When you finish, offer a few words of gratitude—for the task itself, for your capable hands, for the magic that allowed it to happen. Blow out the candle or close your eyes for a breath, sealing the intention: that magic is truly present in the everyday.

Journal Prompts

- When was the last time something ordinary felt sacred to you? What made that moment different?
- What small daily act could you turn into a ritual of presence or gratitude?
- Where in your life has magic shown up uninvited—through timing, coincidence, or a sense of knowing?
- How does the idea of tending an inner flame resonate with you right now? What helps your flame burn brighter?

- Write about a time when grief or loss revealed something unexpectedly beautiful or meaningful.
- What creative acts—writing, cooking, gardening, comforting—help you feel most connected to something larger than yourself?
- If Brigid herself were to walk beside you today, what might she bless in your life?

Time to Rise

Magic is the spark that stirs us after a long sleep—the quiet whisper that says, You're still here. It reminds us that every ending carries the seed of beginning, every ember holds the promise of flame.

When we choose to notice everyday magic, we participate in the world's own becoming. Brigid's fire lights the path ahead, guiding us from stillness into movement, from waiting into becoming. The magic we invite back in lifts us. It says, "It's time to rise."

Part Three

Rising

I am not the woman I once was. I am not interested in becoming her again. I am becoming someone new, someone rooted, someone worth knowing.

Alexandra Elle

Several times in my life, I've experienced an inner knowing that felt so real, so pure, and so right, it left zero doubt in my mind.

The evening I knew I was pregnant with my son was one such time.

Meeting John was another.

It happened just before I picked him up for our first date. I was driving around a traffic circle, two turns away from his house, and the knowing washed over me. It said *your life is about to change.*

And it was right.

Before I met John, I had a lot going for me. I was a good mom. I had a few amazing friends who looked out for me. I did good work for my clients. But it was just me. Singular. Operating on my own, regardless of my relationship status.

You know how they say that falling in love feels like fireworks? I thought that was a bunch of hooey until I met John. Because John and I are alchemy—greater than the sum of our parts. And it was obvious from the start.

That doesn't mean our love bloomed whole and complete on that first date. We both had patterns we needed to unlearn. And the excitement and intensity of those early days stirred up all the usual butterflies.

When John's nervous, he talks. It's a quirk of his. He talks about the Civil War and 1960s music trivia. He talks about his childhood. He talks about past relationships. (I had to ask him to stop talking about that one. It got to be a bit much.)

One night, when we were still new, we were snuggling on the couch, and he was talking about everything and nothing, as he does. In the middle of his soliloquy, he said, "I will not marry you." It was completely random, but he said it so emphatically that I was taken aback. Then, as if that wasn't the weirdest thing ever, he went right on talking about nothing in particular.

I thought, *What the heck was that?* I had no intention of marrying again. It was the furthest thing from my mind. But I didn't interrupt him. Not at first. Instead, my brain kept spinning. *Where did that come from? Does he think I'm trying to trap him somehow?*

I thought about how Dave and I had never talked about hard things, and how I'd promised myself that I wouldn't avoid difficult conversations with anyone in the future. And here we were in the future.

He paused to breathe, and I made my move.

"I have to say, that was a pretty weird thing you just said. That you won't marry me. I just want to say that's fine because I'm not planning on marrying you either."

He said, "Okay, good." And we dropped it.

I was very proud of myself. I'd felt something and I hadn't buried it. I spoke my truth. And I meant it.

It didn't take long before all that went out the window. We couldn't deny that our connection was deeper and more special than either of us had experienced before, and the urge to tie yet another knot started to show up. It whispered at first, but it was growing louder.

John had mentioned that he had driven through Tennessee once and thought it was beautiful, so I planned a trip for us. We stayed at a place called Honeymoon Hills. We called it our "practice honeymoon."

While we were in Tennessee, we arranged for a trail ride through the Smoky Mountains. It was beautiful the way that forests are when the weather is overcast and a bit dreary. John was riding ahead of me, single file, on the narrow path, when my inner knowing dropped this on me: *you are going to take his name.*

I'd given up plenty of ground on the whole getting married thing, but one thing I remained firm on was that I was not going to give up my name. I'd already done that twice, and I didn't want to do it again.

And yet, the decision had been made. There was no point in resisting.

When I told John, not only that I wanted to take his name, but when and where I made that decision, he was floored. Then he did something very special. He asked if he could take my name too.

So about a year later, on a rainy day in December, we got married in a civil ceremony at the courthouse in Rockville, Maryland. Just the two of us. And we became Ann Coleman Bevans Landis and John Roger Bevans Landis. We went to a fancy restaurant for our first meal as a married couple, and while we were there, we surprised all of Facebook with our new names.

Yes, I'd been married before. Twice. But this time was different, because I was different. We were different.

Some time later, I asked John what he meant that night when he said he would not marry me. He thought about it for a moment, then said, "I think I was just trying to convince myself."

If descent is unraveling and initiation is listening, rising is the becoming. This is when you begin to weave new patterns out of the threads left in your lap. It's when you begin to choose, step by step, your new life. And those choices may surprise you.

You know you've made it to rising when the universe says, *your life is about to change.*

The Nature of Rising

Rising doesn't look like constant triumph. Sometimes rising looks like saying no to something you would have once agreed to. Sometimes it looks like walking away from what drains you. Sometimes it looks like speaking your truth, even when you're afraid of what it could mean.

Yes or no or maybe. Now or later or never. All choices that shape who you are becoming.

It's a bit like planting season. The seed is pressed into the soil, where it has everything a seed could possibly need. Darkness. Water. Warmth. But it can't stay a seed forever. One day, it breaks through the surface, tender and green. The seedling is not yet strong, but it's reaching for the sun. Rising is like that. Small shoots of new life, fragile but undeniable.

As I emerged from my initiation, I started making different choices. I spoke up when, before, I might have stayed quiet. I walked away from projects I kept working on just because I was afraid to disappoint anyone. I learned how to let things be as they were and change when they needed to, without clinging to what was or what might have been.

For the first time, I started questioning the assumption that perfection was the only way to be good enough, and that control meant safety. I began to apply all the things I'd learned during my initiation. I started to ask what life could be.

Rewriting the Rules

To rise, you must rewrite the rules that once bound you. The rules that said you must be good, pleasing, productive, selfless. The rules that told you your worth was measured by what you achieved or how you looked.

Sometimes, when you really think about it, you realize that you've been living by so many unexamined rules that it's astonishing you function at all. You're like a tin man, bound up by the rust of conflicting directives.

Rising is about letting go of old rules and crafting new ones rooted in truth. I will rest when I am tired. I will speak when I have something to say. I will no longer apologize for existing.

This is not selfishness. It is sovereignty. It is remembering that your life is yours to shape.

Becoming Her

During your rising, there's a moment when you glimpse the woman you are becoming. Not the girl you were, not the mask you wore, but the self who has been waiting all along.

For me, she appeared one afternoon at a horse rescue where I was a volunteer. It struck me how much I loved the feeling of pulling hoses and scrubbing troughs and scooping manure. No one was watching. No one was grading me. I was alive, joyful, present, and doing what I loved. I thought, *if only I could do this, all day every day, I would be so happy.* I surprised myself with that thought, then I surprised myself even more by taking it seriously.

Becoming her is not a single moment but a continual unfolding. Each day you choose again to live in alignment, to honor your body, to trust your knowing. Slowly, the woman you are becoming emerges more fully.

The Life You Would Allow Yourself to Live

Perhaps the most radical part of rising is giving yourself permission to live the life you've always longed for. To choose joy over obligation. To create beauty for its own sake.

This isn't fantasy. It's practice. Each choice becomes a stitch in the fabric of a new life. The more you practice, the stronger the weave becomes.

One day I opened my eyes and saw that the little girl who splashed through the mud every Saturday morning and wrote poems about horses had become a woman who fretted over client invoices and started stories, but never finished them.

I thought my dreams were only dreams. Until one day I realized they were treasure, and my life was the map.

The Chapters Ahead

In this part of the book, we will rise together.

In Chapter 7, we'll identify and release the scripts that kept us small and claim the authority to shape new ones. You'll begin to replace old patterns of striving and self-doubt with truths that honor your strength, your rhythm, and your right to take up space.

In Chapter 8, we'll explore what it means to embody the woman you are becoming, not in theory but in daily practice. Through rituals, reflection, and gentle acts of courage, you'll learn to live from your center and make choices that reflect who you truly are—not who the world told you to be.

In Chapter 9, we'll craft visions of what it looks like to live in freedom, joy, and alignment. This is where you step fully into the life you've been preparing for, one built from your values, nourished by your joy, and guided by your own sacred knowing.

Invitation

Rising is not about becoming someone else. It's about becoming more fully yourself. It's about allowing the truths revealed in unraveling and initiation to mature and bear fruit.

You are not the woman you once were, and you are not meant to be. You are becoming someone else, someone rooted, someone who has always been worthy.

Let this be the season you stand tall in your own life. Let this be the season you rise.

Chapter 7

Rewrite the Rules

When I was a kid, life had a soundtrack.

Both of my parents had little songs they would sing to us, refrains that invariably made my sister and me roll our eyes.

One of Mom's favorites was the line, "I'm so sorry, Uncle Albert." She'd sing this to us whenever we wanted something she wasn't prepared to give. I was well into my forties before I learned it was a line from a real song by Paul and Linda McCartney.

Dad's song was even more grating. He would sing,

R-E-S
P-O-N
S-I-bility

I won't burden you with the tune. But when I think of my childhood, that song rings in my ears.

For my dad, lots of things fell under the mantle of "responsibility." Earning exceptional grades. Having perfect manners. Always doing your homework. Committing to hobbies you've tried once. Never needing help with an assignment. Practicing music every day.

If I brought home a 98% on a test, he would ask, "What happened to the other two points?" Anything worse than that would trigger the song.

At least half the time, Dad thought he was being funny when he said these things. But comments made in jest don't always land that way in children. At least, they didn't land that way in me.

To my young mind, the cardinal rules were these:

1. Be perfect.
2. If you're not perfect, for God's sake, don't let anyone find out about it.

It's easy to see how those rules could have played out in all sorts of situations. Like covering up my mother's alcoholism, for example. That secret was buried so deep that some of her closest relatives didn't know she had a problem until the day she died.

Growing up, I navigated the rules by giving up activities that didn't please my parents (like horses) and adopting activities that did (like music).

I never absorbed the rules that other people were born knowing, like what to say or not say, what to do or not do, and how to behave so you'll be accepted. Consequently, I was always saying and doing the wrong thing at the wrong time—at home and at school.

The best solution I could come up with was to fly under the radar, focusing on being the perfect student and slipping by unnoticed in social situations. I also developed a habit of extreme independence and refused to ask for help, no matter how bad things got. It was a vicious cycle of isolation, invisibility and shame.

I carried my parents' rules with me into my adult life, and it wasn't pretty. I tried to be the perfect daughter, the perfect wife, the perfect employee. Three years into my first marriage, my body broke down hard. I couldn't sleep and I was suffering from debilitating pain. It was the opening volley of a lifelong war with fibromyalgia.

In short, it felt like the instructions everyone else received for how to fit in were written in a language I didn't understand. And the rules my parents gave me—be perfect or be invisible—just made it worse.

During my initiation, I finally made the space I needed to observe the mechanics of my own life. All the shame I had accumulated from a lifetime of doing everything "wrong" became visible. And my heavy heart, which I had wrapped in bandages and barbed wire, began to beat again.

I learned that I didn't have to feel stuck, constrained by someone else's rules. That I could stand up for myself and my truth, just like Arachne.

Meet Arachne

In a quiet valley in Lydia, where sheep grazed on hillsides, brushed by thyme and wind, there lived a girl whose hands seemed made for weaving. Her name was Arachne, and she was the daughter of a humble shepherd and dyer of wool. Her father spent his days among the sheep, shearing and carding the fleece, then dipping it into vats of crimson and violet.

From the time she could walk, Arachne was captivated by the rhythm of his work—the soft rasp of combed wool, the hiss of steam, the smell of lanolin and dye. The first time she touched a spindle, it was as if something ancient stirred inside her. She wove as other children played—with delight, devotion, and an instinct so pure it seemed older than the hills.

Her cloth shimmered with life. Flowers, faces, and constellations unfurled beneath her fingers. Travelers passing through her village carried her name to the cities, then to the temples, until whispers reached even Olympus itself: *a mortal who weaves as well as a goddess.*

When Athena, goddess of wisdom and craft, heard this, she descended to Lydia disguised as an old woman. She found Arachne at her loom, sunlight catching in the threads, a half-finished tapestry spilling from her lap like water.

"You weave beautifully," said the old woman. "But you must thank Athena, who gave mortals the art of weaving."

Arachne looked up from her work, her eyes clear and unwavering. "I learned from no goddess," she said. "My skill is my own."

The old woman straightened, her disguise dissolving in a shimmer of light. Athena stood tall and terrible, her gray eyes gleaming like storm clouds.

"Then prove it," the goddess said. "Let us weave, and let the truth decide."

They placed their looms side by side. Athena's tapestry sang with divine order: Zeus on his throne, heroes kneeling in reverence, the perfection of Olympus unchallenged.

Arachne's, though, told another story. She wove the gods' misdeeds. Their vanity, their cruelty, their endless hunger for worship. Her threads burned with color and truth.

When the final thread was tied, even Athena could find no flaw. Arachne's tapestry was perfect. And that perfection cut deeper than any insult. The goddess' face hardened. In a burst of rage, she tore Arachne's work apart. The loom splintered. The threads scattered.

"How dare you mock Olympus?" she thundered.

Arachne stood her ground. Her heart pounded, but she did not bow. "I did not mock you," she said. "I told the truth. If that offends the gods, perhaps the gods should change."

Athena's eyes flashed like lightning. Arachne knew her defiance was dangerous, but still she stood by her truth. She did not cry out or beg. She reached for the ruined threads at her feet, as if to begin again.

Athena raised her hand. "Then weave forever," she said.

And with that, Arachne's body began to change. Her arms lengthened, her fingers multiplied, her form grew small and light. She became the first spider, condemned by the goddess to spin without rest, her brilliance turned to endless labor.

The goddess vanished, leaving only the wind and the faint shimmer of silk.

But the story did not end there.

They say Arachne still spins in the quiet hours, her web catching the morning light like threads of gold. Some call it punishment. Others see it for what it is—a kind of victory. Her weaving endures long after Athena's has turned to dust.

Arachne refused to yield, and for that, she became eternal. She rewrote the rule that said creation must serve power. Her tapestry was destroyed, but her truth remains—woven into the air itself.

When you see a spider's web glistening at dawn, remember her. Remember that some rules must be broken, and some gifts must be claimed. Weave anyway.

Choosing Your Own Thread

For most of my life, I believed the rules were already written.

That they lived outside of me, handed down by people who claimed to know better—parents, teachers, bosses, partners, the "grown-ups in the room." I thought my job was to follow them perfectly, or at least convincingly, and pray no one ever noticed how much I was struggling underneath the performance.

But when I look back now, I can see how shaky those rules really were. They weren't cosmic. They weren't universal. They weren't even kind. They were simply the expectations that started with two imperfect parents doing the best they could with the tools they had. I treated those rules like gospel, and I saw them everywhere.

Arachne's story reminds us what happens when we see the truth. The rules aren't sacred. They're stitched together by human hands, and they can be unstitched just as easily.

Arachne didn't defy a goddess because she wanted attention or glory. She did it because something inside her said, *No, this is mine. This is who I am. This is how I was made.*

There's something holy in that kind of devotion to your own voice.

Most of us don't need to challenge Olympus, but we do need to challenge the old, brittle rules that tell us to make ourselves small.

We need to question the voices that still echo from childhood. The ones that insist perfection is safety, invisibility is protection, and needing help is weakness.

And at some point, we have to do what Arachne did—sit down at the loom of our own life and choose what thread comes next.

Not the thread of performance. Not the thread of fear. Not the thread of someone else's comfort. But the thread that feels like truth in our hands.

Because the moment we stop trying to earn our place and start weaving from who we really are—something shifts. Shame loosens, the heart softens, and a new pattern appears, one we didn't know we were capable of making.

This is what rewriting the rules looks like.

Not rebellion for rebellion's sake, but the quiet, unmistakable decision to honor the life that was always trying to emerge through us.

Arachne didn't lose her power. She transformed. She became unstoppable.

And so can you.

A Discovery and a Loss

Not long after I admitted to myself that I am not a musician, I began to ask, "If not that, then what?"

One afternoon, John and I were sitting side by side on the couch scrolling our phones. He said, "There's a post here asking for volunteers to help take care of horses at a rescue."

We had been married for about a year and a half and had moved out of our little apartment to a rented craftsman bungalow next to Catoctin National Park. We were scratching an itch for more space, and the little house on one acre was a move in the right direction. We called it our Steppingstone Cottage.

It was late summer, and there was a pile of zucchinis on the dining room table that had come from our vegetable garden. They all had little bites taken out of them, thanks to our two abundantly curious cats.

"Where's the rescue?" I asked.

"It says it's in Thurmont."

Thurmont was the next town over.

I had already begun thinking about buying a place where we could keep horses, but I'd never actually taken care of them before. I'd only ever taken riding lessons. Volunteering at a rescue seemed like a good way to learn the ropes and help a good cause at the same time.

A few days later, I found myself scooping feed into buckets under the watchful eye of Sharon Burrier, the founder of Rocky's Horse Rescue and Rehabilitation.

It felt so good to spend time with horses again. It was different from taking lessons. I got to know all of their personalities and quirks. I also heard their tragic stories. Some were owner surrenders, horses who were well-cared for, but for whatever reason, their owners couldn't keep them anymore. Others escaped a tragic end in the kill pen, where they would have been sold for slaughter if Rocky's hadn't stepped in.

The horses were all carefully rehabilitated. The older and sicker ones were retired at Rocky's or fostered by supporters, but the younger and healthier ones were trained or retrained and adopted out to loving homes.

There are many legitimate non-profit horse rescues around the country. If this speaks to you, I encourage you to learn more.

One of the horses at the rescue was a beautiful pinto with one blue eye called Betty. The first day I met her, Betty decided I was her person. She followed me around while I did my chores, and I stopped here and there to tell her she was a pretty girl and to give her scratches.

From then on, when she saw my car coming up the drive, she and her friend Holly would run over to the fence and whinny at me. I told Betty that she and Holly and I were squadies. Betty always got an extra cookie from me in her food bucket.

During the pandemic, I eventually came down with COVID. I had to take two weeks off to recover. On my first day back, I walked into the barn and said, "Hey guys, I'm back!" Betty led eight horses and one mule in a jubilant chorus of neighs.

I volunteered two or three times per week, and I always left the rescue with my heart full. I wanted to tell everyone about all of the beautiful souls I was caring for, and for a while, there wasn't much else I'd talk about.

My dad was in nursing care by then, and he heard me gush about the rescue as much as anyone. The first few times, he feigned interest, but on each visit, he was less and less invested until, finally, he said, "well, you always liked that stuff."

By "that stuff," he meant being outdoors, taking care of animals, and getting dirt under my fingernails. "That stuff" was the antithesis of his stuff. It always had been.

The comment was his signal to change the subject, but to be honest, I'd never felt more seen by my own father. He noticed, all those years ago, that I loved a thing. And that was something.

Then again, he noticed, but he didn't really care. It was frivolous to him. A waste of time. A subject to be changed.

I kept talking about the horses, because that's really all I had to talk about. And also, because I knew it annoyed him just a little. That was me, standing up for my truth. Not to Athena. To somebody tougher. My dad.

During the last few weeks of Dad's life, my sister and I visited him frequently (as did John and Avery, who also loved him and were absolute angels during that time). As his health continued to deteriorate, my fellow volunteers offered to take my shifts at the rescue. But there was nowhere else I wanted to be. Horses see your energy. Brushing them, talking to them, and crying into their fluffy winter coats held me together in a way that other humans, no matter how well-intentioned, could not.

The day before Dad died, I went to see him in the hospital. His delirium had taken over, but I knew he could feel my cool hand on his forehead. I told him it was all going to be okay and that his loved ones were waiting for him. Then I told him a secret I hadn't told anyone—that the last thing I said to Mom the night she died was to promise her I would take care of Dad until he was ready to go home. That night, with my hand on his forehead, I told him that she would take it from there.

Later that night, as I slept fitfully two hours away, my sister-in-law Avery woke up. It was 3:30 in the morning, and she had a thought that was not her own: *I need to pray for Dad.*

A few minutes later, I got the call that he had died.

My dad was complicated. Funny, generous, and fiercely proud my sister and me, even if he didn't always understand our choices. He was grateful for every moment we spent with him during those last few years, whether we were cruising down the Danube, catching an Orioles game, or losing track of him in the grocery store.

Our relationship had its ups and downs, but I'm glad I got to call him Dad.

A Breaking Point

When Dad died, I had been working as a self-employed web developer for more than 20 years. I'd never gotten the Master's degree he wanted me to get, nor the PhD. I'd never played 'cello in a major symphony either.

It weighed on me over the years, when I thought about how far my life had strayed from the path my parents had laid out for me. I knew they were disappointed in me at times. They certainly didn't have three husbands on their bingo card. *Maybe I should have listened,* I thought. *Maybe I should have done it their way. It would have been easier.*

But then I thought about the last job I had. Long days at the office, writing the same proposal over and over again. The same differentiation factors. The same past performance. The same references. As my own boss, every project I accepted brought with it the promise of learning something new. That was important to me. So I tried hard to keep up appearances, to make it sound like everything was going great. Even when it wasn't.

Every few years, when things got especially tight, I'd think about getting a real job. One with a steady paycheck, paid time off, and a 401(k). But the older I got, the less my resume matched what employers were looking for. Blazing my own trail had become a trap.

The whole thing was complicated by the fact that, once Dave and I separated, I was the sole breadwinner. I couldn't afford to have a bad month. There was nobody I could go to for help because asking for help violated my internal rules.

So I leaned on my contract position and kept accepting new work. As time went on, I had a harder and harder time keeping up the insane hours all that work required. The stress of the divorce, John's illness, moving to the cottage, and eventually losing my dad frayed my brain more than I realized.

One day I reached a breaking point. We were living in the cottage, and I had too many deadlines piling up. I had steeled myself for an all-nighter. Then the internet went out at 3 a.m. Without access to my web server, there was nothing I could do. And I was hopped up on too much coffee to sleep.

I waited around for a couple of hours, but the pressure was too much. At 5 a.m., I got in the car and drove to one of those gas stations with a giant convenience store and hot food. They were open 24 hours and had free wifi.

I had three major projects going. I would work on one for 45 minutes or an hour, then get an emergency request for another. So I'd switch to that one until something else came up. I went round and round, changing projects so many times that barely anything got done.

At 11:00 am, I couldn't take it anymore. I was beyond my breaking point. I packed up my stuff and drove home. John took one look at me and pulled me into a hug. I was shaking.

With his help, I texted my clients, canceling all my afternoon meetings due to an unspecified medical situation. The medical situation was that I was very close to a nervous breakdown. I crawled into bed. John closed the curtains and held me as I sobbed.

It was a breaking point. I couldn't bear the weight of everything I'd said yes to. I couldn't keep living by the rule that said I had to be perfect or die trying. I had to choose a new thread. Choosing that thread is where we're going next.

Gentle Calls to Action

Begin by noticing the rules you still follow without question. They live in the language of habit—the quiet shoulds and musts that slip out when you're tired or afraid.

> *I should keep it together.*
> *I have to make this work.*
> *That's just how it's done.*

These phrases seem harmless, but they reveal the invisible scaffolding that still shapes your days. As you rise, you begin to see that scaffolding has to go.

When you catch yourself following an old rule, pause long enough to ask who wrote it. Whose comfort does this rule protect? Whose approval does it seek? What fear keeps it alive? So often, these invisible laws were created by someone else—perhaps a parent, a teacher, a culture—and you've carried them long after they stopped serving you.

Once you see them clearly, you can decide which ones still belong in your life. Some may still hold meaning, and that's okay. Others may need to be rewritten, not in rebellion, but in reverence for who you've become and what you know now.

As you unlearn, make space for imperfection. Let yourself stumble, laugh, and begin again. Every time you choose authenticity over performance, you're weaving a new pattern—one with room for breath and softness.

You are the weaver now. You get to decide which threads to carry forward, which to release, and which new colors to spin from your own truth. No one else can write your pattern for you. Only you can decide what belongs.

Ritual Suggestion

Rituals for rewriting the rules don't need to be grand or elaborate. They only need to be intentional. You might begin by gathering a small piece of paper and something to write with. Find a quiet place. A table at your favorite cafe, the porch at dusk, a patch of grass beside a lake. Any place you feel safe will do. Take a few steadying breaths.

Write down one rule that no longer serves you. It might be something you've outgrown, something that keeps you small, or something that was never truly yours to begin with. Don't rush. Let the words come exactly as they need to. When you're ready, read it back and notice what rises in your body—relief, sadness, defiance, maybe even grief. All of it belongs.

When you're ready, fold the paper and hold it gently in your hands. Whisper a few words of gratitude to whoever taught you this rule. They were doing the best they could, and for a time, the rule probably kept you safe. Then, thank yourself for recognizing that safety and freedom don't often go hand in hand.

If it feels right, release the paper. Bury it in the earth, burn it carefully, or tear it into small pieces and scatter them to the wind. As you do, speak a new truth aloud. Something simple, like: *I am free to live by what is real for me now.*

Sit in the quiet for a moment, breathing in the space you've made. Imagine the air around you filling with new threads of color and possibility. This is your new pattern forming—woven from choice, self-trust, and gentle rebellion.

Journal Prompts

- What "invisible rules" still shape how you behave, love, or work?

- Where did those rules come from—and who benefits from you following them?
- What would it feel like to break one of those rules today, just a little?
- In what ways have you mistaken perfection for safety?
- What new rule—or truth—would you like to weave into your life instead?
- How does your body feel when you act from freedom rather than fear?

Your New Rules for Living

When you begin to live by your own rules, the world might not understand at first, but your soul will. The threads you choose now will shimmer with truth, not perfection, and that will hold you steady. Every act of self-trust is a new stitch in the life you're weaving—one that finally belongs to you.

And as you practice living this way, you may find that nothing dramatic happens. Not at first. Instead, the shift comes in subtle ways. An inhale that's deeper than before. A decision that once felt impossible landing softly in your hands. A small, surprising moment of ease. This is how new rules take root: not by force, but by presence. By noticing what feels real, and choosing it again. And again. And again.

Over time, these small choices accumulate. They become a rhythm, or a new internal language. You start to recognize your own voice beneath the noise. You begin to trust the tug of your own thread. And slowly, almost imperceptibly, the life you've been weaving in secret reveals itself in the open—steady, spacious, unmistakably yours.

Chapter 8

Becoming Her

So far, we've let go of our attachment to everything we were taught to be, tuning in to who we really are beneath performance and conditioning. We've opened ourselves to the magic of possibility, and we've rewritten the rules so we might live by our truth.

Together, we've traversed descent and initiation, and now, in our rising, we have arrived at the transformation you've been waiting for. This is the moment when you begin to put all the pieces together.

It's time to become her.

Magic to Do

My dad had an enormous record collection. But he wasn't interested in rock and roll. Among the classical masters and corny showtunes, there were a few albums that captured my imagination.

One was the soundtrack to *Star Wars*. I especially loved the raucous cantina music. I copied it to a cassette and played it during many solo rollerskating sessions in our concrete-floored basement.

Another album that caught my eye when I was eight or nine had a pink jacket with jesters on it. The jesters formed he word *Pippin* with their bodies. It looked interesting to my child eyes, so I put it on the player. It was like nothing I'd ever heard before.

The opening tune of this 1972 Bob Fosse musical is called "Magic To Do." In it, the Leading Player, a role created by stage and screen legend Ben Vereen, sings:

> We got magic to do just for you
> We got miracle plays to play
> We got parts to perform
> Hearts to warm
> Kings and things to take by storm
> As we go along our way

After a few listens, I figured out that Pippin was the only son of the Emperor Charlemagne, the free-spirited heir to the throne, a dreamer who just couldn't fit in to court life. Early in the first act, Pippin sings:

> Everything has its season
> Everything has its time
> Show me a reason and I'll soon show you a rhyme
> Cats fit on the windowsill
> Children fit in the snow
> Why do I feel I don't fit in anywhere I go?

Even at that tender age, I could relate.

The album that looked so kid-friendly on its cover (spoiler: it's really not) had a lot to say about how to live a creative life, how to find your place in the world, and how extraordinary love can be found in everyday things.

It was my own personal soundtrack. I imagined I was the woman in "Love Song." When things got hard, I listened to the Player's encouraging words in "On the Right Track" or sang along to "No Time at All." And most of all, I commiserated with Pippin, as he sang:

> The fact that I'm special is easy to see
> So why doesn't anybody see it but me?
> I'm extraordinary
> I need to do extraordinary things

That's the trap, isn't it? He sings this near the end, during his final push, when he's at his most insistent. Just before he realizes what life is really about.

I have listened to that album at least 1,000 times. From the beginning, I recognized how strongly it resonated with me. What I didn't understand until much later was that it was a breadcrumb, one of many clues scattered throughout my life, that hinted at my purpose.

It finally dawned on me years later when I was undertaking a rebrand of my software company. I thought long and hard about what my business was really about. At last it came to me: *software is magic*.

It's magic because no one but the programmer understands what's going on under the hood. When it's done well, the user doesn't stop to think about all the loops and conditional statements and error handling that had to be coded. To the user, it just works.

We call it a black box. You put stuff in one end, and something better comes out the other. If that isn't magic, I'm not sure what is.

From there, the clues fell into place like tumblers in a lock:

> A stranger's determination to give Dad communion.
> A call for volunteers in John's Facebook feed.
> An unexpected court filing that saved his life.
> Sandee's phone number ablaze in my mind.
> A promise I made to my mother.
> Counting the tiles in the ultrasound room.

Conceiving my child in a doctor's office.
Getting laid off from my job.
My grandfather's advice.
The Sound and the Fury.
Cantering in France.
Table B.
Larasa.
Longe line.
And through it all, *Pippin.*

All of it mattered. All of it magic.

That's when I knew my purpose: I came here with magic to do.

You too have left clues for yourself. And only you can put them back together. But first you have to find them.

Meet Isis

A long time ago, when the desert wind still carried the breath of creation, the sky goddess Nut and the earth god Geb had four children: Osiris, Isis, Set, and Nephthys.

The younger daughter, Isis, was sharp-minded, tender-hearted, and radiant. Even as a child, she had a gift for seeing what others overlooked. She saw how the reeds bent to the river, how the moon called the tides, how the human heart, fragile yet fierce, longed for love and belonging.

From the beginning, Isis was a weaver of worlds.

When she and her brother Osiris grew older, they married, as gods sometimes do. Together, they brought harmony to the land. Osiris ruled with fairness, and Isis walked among the people, teaching them how to grind grain, heal wounds, soothe fevers, and plant seeds in the dark earth along the Nile. Under their care, Egypt flourished.

But not everyone rejoiced at this. Their brother, Set, grew jealous of the love Osiris inspired and the tenderness Isis brought to the world. He hungered for power.

One night, Set offered Osiris a beautiful chest made of cedar and inlaid with gold. It was a gift, he said. A tribute. A token of brotherly affection.

But it was a trap.

Set invited Osiris to step inside the chest to admire its craftsmanship and, when he did, Set slammed the lid shut and sealed it with molten lead. He cast the coffin into the Nile and watched the river swallow it whole.

When Isis heard what had happened, she did not grieve. Instead, she rose to her full height, the air around her shimmering with purpose. Because Isis was the kind of woman who would cross worlds for what she loved.

She searched the riverbanks and the reed beds and the edges of the desert. She asked stones and trees and birds if they had seen the chest. She asked the wind to carry her voice farther.

Days became weeks. Weeks became months. But Isis did not stop. She was guided by something deeper than hope—something ancient and unyielding. Her inner knowing told her that what is truly yours cannot be lost, only scattered.

At last she found the coffin lodged in the roots of a tall tamarisk tree. Inside lay Osiris—still, serene, untouched by time. Isis wept then, not from weakness but from relief. She cut him free, carried him home, and hid him among the marshes until she could restore him fully.

But Set discovered her secret. In a final act of violence, he tore Osiris apart, scattering his body across Egypt—fragments of a god flung to the corners of the earth.

What Set did not understand was this: a woman who knows who she is cannot be stopped so easily.

Isis set out again, this time walking the map of her grief. She crossed villages and mountains, deserts and riverbanks, gathering every fragment. Each piece she found, she washed with milk and tears. She sang over them. She reassembled him with the patience of a woman rebuilding her own heart.

With the help of Nephthys and Anubis, Isis stitched Osiris back together, not as he once was, but as something new: a god of rebirth, lord of the underworld, keeper of the mysteries of transformation.

Reunited, the lovers conceived their son Horus—the child of restoration. A future born from remembering.

They say that, from that day forward, Isis became the most revered goddess in all of Egypt—not because she was the most powerful, but because she was devoted. Because she understood the truth at the center of every transformation:

> What is lost can be found.
> What is broken can be remade.
> And what is scattered can be gathered back into wholeness.

Becoming the Woman You Were Meant To Be

This sacred journey began when you stopped trying to force yourself into someone else's shape. As you rise, now is the time to gather all your lost parts—the parts that make up the woman you were always meant to become.

This is rarely a sudden transformation. It unfolds across time, as Isis walked the length of Egypt collecting the scattered pieces of her love. It requires patience, tenderness, and a steady devotion that feels almost instinctual.

We all left parts of ourselves behind as we grew up. We set aside the dreams that didn't make sense to the adults around us. We loosened our grip on the passions that weren't practical, acceptable, or convenient. We buried the longings that weren't met with enthusiasm. But even buried, those early loves don't disappear. They wait, just below the surface, until we are finally old enough, brave enough, or exhausted enough to go back and find them.

This is the work of becoming. Not reinvention, but remembrance. It's the gradual recognition that the girl you once were wasn't naïve or silly or unrealistic; she was true. She was the purest version of your instincts, your joy, and your creative force. When you bend down to reclaim even one fragment of what she carried, something inside you clicks back into place. Not all at once, and not perfectly, but unmistakably.

Isis teaches us that wholeness is built piece by piece. It comes from honoring what you loved before the world told you who to be. It comes from trusting that the parts of yourself you abandoned for survival are still yours to reclaim. It comes from understanding that you don't become a new woman in midlife—you become a truer one.

As you gather these pieces, your life takes on a new shape. One that feels both familiar and surprising. You start to see that your childhood passions were never accidents. They were clues. Doorways. Invitations. And when you follow them now, with the wisdom you've earned and the agency you've gained, you are not returning to the past. You're stepping fully into yourself, right here and now.

This is the quiet grace of becoming her—the woman your younger self always hoped you'd grow into, and the woman your future self already knows you can be.

Becoming Me

I've written quite a bit about how much I loved horses, how I lost them, and how I found them again. But there's so much more to the story.

When I was 15 years old, my parents put me on a Greyhound bus (by myself!) and sent me to Waynesboro, Virginia, a small town nestled in the foothills of the Blue Ridge Mountains. I went there to spend three weeks with my friend Caroline.

Caroline and I met in fifth grade. She was the new kid, and the only empty desk in the room was next to mine. That first day, she didn't know I was the weirdest, most bullied kid in the whole school, so she gave me a chance. It turned out she also loved horses, and we became fast friends.

A few years later, Caroline's parents bought a small farm in Waynesboro. Improbably, Caroline and I kept in touch. Email and social media had yet to be invented, and long distance phone calls were very expensive, so we recorded messages to each other on cassette tapes and sent them back and forth through the mail. We were ahead of our time.

The family had a few acres—enough room for a couple of horses, a small orchard, an apiary with four hives, and a big vegetable garden. During my stay, we had a blast, riding horses, tubing down the creek, walking along railroad tracks, wandering around Roses department store, and getting into a little bit of trouble, as 15-year-old girls sometimes do. I felt so at home with her family. I didn't want to leave.

As the return Greyhound loomed, I remember standing by the house, looking out over the garden and the apiary and the little barn. I thought, "This is perfect. I want a place just like it one day." And I meant it.

But life had other plans.

Twenty-eight years later, I came up for air. I had all but forgotten about the little farm at the base of the mountain. All I knew was that I had spent a long time not being myself, and I finally had a chance to choose again.

At first, I thought I would travel the world as a digital nomad. Then I met John, and everything changed.

As we shared the stories of our lives, I told him about the little farm in Virginia and the decision I'd made so long ago. For the first time in a long time, it felt possible.

One day, I was browsing Zillow and found a property in Tennessee—a place we loved—that had everything we wanted. Comically so. It had a house, a barn, and a wood shop, but it also had a driving range and a shed built especially for motorcycles, both hobbies we'd dabbled in. It felt like a sign. I said, "We need to go see this place."

When we arrived with our realtor a few days later, we were met by a disheveled man in an undershirt and boxer shorts. He had no idea why we were there. It turned out he was the ex-husband of the owner, who also lived on the property.

Eventually we got a tour. The Zillow listing neglected to mention that the farm had no running water and no well—just a rain collection system that they used for everything, including cooking and bathing. The house had a composting toilet, but they mostly used the outhouse. Then the owner told us a story about *that time she kidnapped her grandson*.

Driving away from that place felt like escaping from *Deliverance*.

We'd come a long way on a whim, so when the realtor said, "There's another place I can show you," we said "why not?" It was so much more than I had ever envisioned. The farm was over 100 acres and it had pasture, farmland, some woods, and a small quarry. The house was more like a shack, and we had no idea how we would get internet out there, but it was beautiful. Impulsively, we made an offer, and it was accepted. At home, I smiled at my reminder on the refrigerator: *expect miracles.*

Around that time, I had a reading with my friend Sita, who is clairvoyant. She looked at me like she was measuring her words and said, "Don't be in too much of a hurry to get to the farm."

I laughed. "Why not?"

"Just don't," she replied.

Shortly thereafter, everything went sideways. The appraisal couldn't be completed because aggressive bees were living in the electrical panel of the house. Since the house didn't appraise, the financing fell through. And then the coup de grace: John was diagnosed with cancer.

It was a heartbreaking turn of events, but we had to focus on John's health, so we put it all down. Instead of moving to Tennessee, we moved to Steppingstone Cottage.

Looking back on how it all unfolded, I am so grateful. Because that beautiful property fell through, we stayed in Maryland, which meant more time with Samson and our young niece. It also mean that we were close by when Dad's health began to fail. Being with him at the end of his life allowed me to keep the last promise I made to my mother.

Fortunately, a dream delayed is not a dream denied. After my Dad passed away, another window opened. John and I were both volunteering at the rescue by then, and we'd started taking riding lessons. That little farm I'd dreamed about felt more and more within reach.

Sitting on the couch in Steppingstone Cottage, I opened Zillow. A listing popped up for a 10-acre farm in a little Pennsylvania town called East Berlin. I noticed it because it was very close to a saddlery we had visited just a few weeks prior. We hadn't been looking in

Pennsylvania, but the listing looked promising. I called our realtor and we went to see it the next day.

I wanted to love that farm. On paper, it was perfect. It had a house, a barn, and a wood shop. But the pastures weren't fenced, and there was a cell phone tower on the property. The log home sounded charming in the listing, but in reality it was small and dark. It just wasn't for us.

Seeing another not-quite-right property was discouraging. But when we got home that night, I pulled up Zillow again. There was a new listing. The photos where stunning. It was an 1834 farmhouse, built entirely out of stone, sitting on 10 acres. It had a beautiful stone bank barn, several other outbuildings, and fenced pasture. It even had a 1/4 acre vineyard. It was located in Abbottstown, PA, less than five miles from the place we had just seen.

Breadcrumbs—the saddlery, the house in East Berlin, and now this—delivered at exactly the right moment.

The first time I walked into that 200-year-old stone and timber barn, I knew we had found the very place I'd always dreamed of, my own version of Caroline's Waynesboro farm, our forever home. We named it Undertree Farm.

Gentle Calls to Action

Begin by noticing what still calls to you. Not the loud demands of daily life, but the soft, persistent tug at the edges of your awareness. The thing you think about in quiet moments, the dream you've talked yourself out of so many times you've nearly forgotten it was yours. Let yourself turn toward it with curiosity rather than judgment. Ask, "What part of me is this? What have I been missing?" You don't need an answer right away. Simply acknowledging the pull is a way of saying yes to your own becoming.

Then give yourself permission to wander back through the memories that shaped you. Revisit the moments when you felt most alive or most yourself, even if they seem small or impractical now. You are not trying to recreate the past—you are gathering the threads a younger you left behind. As you remember, notice what stirs in your body. Pay attention to the warmth, the ache, the flutter of recognition. These sensations are clues. They are the breadcrumbs you scattered for yourself so you could follow them when the time was right.

As you begin to collect these pieces, move slowly. Treat your discoveries with tenderness. You are not cataloging your life; you are welcoming yourself home. Take one small step toward something that feels true—a few minutes spent reliving an old joy, a conversation with someone who once knew you well, a quiet practice that reconnects you to your own magic. Let these steps be imperfect and unhurried.

And as you walk this path, allow yourself to trust the timing. Transformation almost always unfolds the way Isis gathered Osiris—one piece at a time, with patience, devotion, and a willingness to believe that what you thought was lost is still within reach. Let each tiny act of remembering affirm that your life is not moving away from you but toward you.

Finally, open the door for what wants to enter next. You don't have to know the shape of the woman you are becoming; you only have to make space for her. Create moments of stillness where she can breathe through you. Invite a bit of the old magic back in—a spark of wonder, a touch of play, a willingness to see meaning where you once saw coincidence. Each time you do, you step more fully into your truth. You gather another piece. You become a little more whole.

Ritual Suggestion

Choose a time when you can be alone for a few minutes. Sit somewhere comfortable and let the space settle around you. Light a candle if that feels natural, but don't force it. This isn't about ceremony; it's about attention.

Hold something small from your past—a photo, a book you once loved, a piece of jewelry, anything that connects you to an earlier version of yourself. Hold it without trying to feel anything in particular. Just notice what comes up: a memory, a sensation, a question, or nothing at all. All of it is information.

Take a slow breath and ask yourself, "What part of me did I leave here?" Don't dig for an answer. Let your heart offer whatever rises on its own, even if it feels vague or incomplete.

When you're ready, set the object down and say: "I'm willing to bring this part of myself back." Not a promise, not a vow, just willingness.

Blow out the candle, stand up, and go on with your day. The ritual isn't in what you did; it's in the fact that you made a little space for yourself. That's enough.

Journal Prompts

- What part of myself have I been missing, and how do I know it's still there?
- What small moment from my past keeps resurfacing, and what might it be trying to remind me of?
- When did I last feel genuinely like myself, and what was different about that version of me?

- What have I talked myself out of wanting, and what would happen if I let myself want it again?
- Which childhood passion or instinct still pulses under the surface of my life?
- What feels like a breadcrumb—a clue I've left myself without realizing it?
- Where in my life am I ready to reclaim something I set down too early?
- If I imagined gathering one forgotten piece of myself today, what might it be?

Becoming, Step By Step

Becoming her isn't a dramatic leap or a sudden unveiling. It's a slow, steady return to the truths you've carried all along.

As you gather the pieces you once set aside, you start to recognize yourself again—not the version shaped by expectation or survival, but the one who existed before you learned to doubt your own instincts. Each remembered joy, each reclaimed fragment, brings you a little closer to the woman you were always meant to grow into.

And the more you allow her to surface, the more clearly you can feel her presence in your everyday life. Quiet, capable, and already here, waiting for you to step forward.

Chapter 9

The Life You Would Allow Yourself to Live

What kind of life would you allow yourself to live if you truly believed you were worthy of it?

Not the life others laid out for you. Not the life that looks tidy on paper. The life that feels like the greatest expression of your true self.

This question is both exciting and terrifying, because it forces you to confront the gap between your dreams and what you allow. To answer it, you'll need every shred of self-knowledge you've gained since you crossed the threshold and began your descent.

The life you would allow yourself to live is unlikely to materialize fully formed, like armored Athena springing from Zeus's head. (Right after Zeus swallowed her pregnant mother, Metis. What did I say about the myths?)

No, in an extraordinary show of devotion, you will have to build your new life one choice at a time. Many of those choices will be difficult. Perhaps unthinkable. But necessary.

The good news is that the universe has your back. When you're actively making choices that lead you toward your dreams, doors will open that you didn't even know existed. But you have to make the first move.

Don't forget to pack your self-compassion too. Because the road to the life you would allow yourself to live is like a dusty country lane that bends around crooked property lines and dry stream beds. They don't have many road signs out there, so you can expect to make a few wrong turns.

As you undertake this journey, remind yourself that the life you would allow yourself to live is yours and yours alone. There is not, nor has there ever been, nor will there ever be anyone else who can live it but you.

Home

The day we stepped onto the Undertree Farm as its caretakers, not just hopeful visitors, John and I walked through the old house like we'd never seen it before. Inside the massive stone walls, the rooms were empty, but they held the energy of so many who had come before.

We later learned the house was built in stages. The oldest part, built in 1800, was once a single room with a large cooking hearth. A narrow staircase curled into a small attic. Its treads were worn by thousands upon thousands of footfalls. It's impossible to know when the original one-room house was last updated, but the broad plank, honey-colored floor suggests it was a long time ago.

At some point, the hearth was converted into a big closet with cabinets on either side. John reached into one of those cabinets and pulled out an old squeeze box that someone, many generations earlier, had left behind. He accompanied himself as he made up a song on the spot—a gentle greeting to let the house know we were home.

As we moved from room to room, making plans and lists, it dawned on me that it had all come true. Not all at once. The farm was the ultimate expression of my dream, but it started years earlier at Steppingstone Cottage when we practiced planting vegetables in our little garden, and before that when we had a container garden on the balcony of our apartment, and before that when Caroline's mother showed me how to weed a bed, and before that when I shelled peas for my mother at our backyard picnic table. It started the first time I made yeast bread, and before that when I used all those kitty-approved zucchinis to make my mother's famous Chocolate Zucchini Cake, and before that the first time I was in charge of Thanksgiving dinner, and before that when my mother taught me to make chocolate chip cookies from scratch.

There it was again. That breadcrumb feeling. It had all led to this. It was impossible, but here we were, talking about the torn wallpaper in the kitchen. And I felt nothing but grateful.

Over the next few weeks, we carefully arranged our belongings, which we had collected over many years. My solid wood dining table, a gift from my father, fit perfectly in the dining room. John placed a smaller table, which he had found by the side of the road years earlier, in the game room. As movers wriggled my secretary up the stairs to the master bedroom, I said, "Be careful! Not because it's fragile. Because it's haunted." I think they knew I was serious because they moved a little quicker after that.

I thought about all the choices that led John and me to each other and to our farm. Ending a other relationships. Starting over financially. Getting married, even though neither one of us thought we wanted that. Moving to Steppingstone Cottage. And those were just a few of the big ones. Perhaps the first step was both the smallest and the most consequential: we both said yes to a crab feast.

It wasn't smooth sailing. Sometimes we suffered at the hand of fate, like when John was diagnosed with cancer. Sometimes we chose to pursue things that led us away from the path for a little while before we found our way back, like the farm in Tennessee. But looking back at everything that happened, I don't see how it could have unfolded any other way.

One of our first improvements to the farm was a three-stall run-in shed. A few days after it was delivered, Sharon brought us two foster horses from Rocky's—Buddy and Popeye. Buddy was an elder paint who had always been a little sweet on me. Popeye was a retired Belgian draft horse who had recently lost his partner, Ben.

The field hadn't been grazed in a long time. We turned them loose and they bounced around gleefully, for all the world looking like much younger horses, stopping here and there to pull up a mouthful of green grass.

That first night, John and I sat on the porch watching them. "I can't believe I finally have horses," I said. "I've been waiting my whole life for this." Then I turned to John and asked, "Will they stay?" As if the fence wasn't high enough or strong enough to contain a dream I had dreamed for so long.

A winding path. Perfectly timed steps and distractions in equal measure. And ultimately, a resting place that was better than we'd dared to dream.

If there were ever a person who would understand the complex interplay between choice, fate, and timing, it was Atalanta.

Meet Atalanta

The day Atalanta was born, her father abandoned her on a mountainside because he believed a daughter wasn't worth keeping. She should have died of exposure or hunger or loneliness, but nature made space for her.

A bear came across the tiny pink newborn and raised her as one of her cubs. The bear didn't treat her as fragile or ornamental as a human parent might have. Instead, the mother bear taught her to stay warm, follow scent, and move with both caution and confidence.

Atalanta grew up in the wild, running through the forest and learning to trust her instincts instead of burying them. She belonged to the Earth, exploring during the day and sleeping on soft pine needles at night.

By the time human hunters found her, she wasn't helpless or timid. She was a small, fierce thing who knew how to survive. The men could have taken her home and tried to turn her into a proper girl, reshaping her into what society expected. But they saw something in her that gave them pause. Instead of dragging her back to the human world, they taught her to use a bow, to track animals, and to move silently through the forest. She became skilled, not because she was trying to impress anyone, but because she delighted in what her body could do.

Atalanta's childhood was remarkable for what it left out: there was no pressure to be pretty, agreeable, or accommodating. No one told her to shrink herself. No one warned her that toughness would make her unlovable. She grew up without the endless commentary most girls receive about how to behave, how to look, and how to fit into a world that demands softness and sacrifice.

By the time she returned to her father's house as an adult, Atalanta was known as the fastest runner in Greece and one of its most skilled archers. Approval meant nothing to her. But her father didn't see the woman she had become. He saw an opportunity. A daughter like Atalanta could elevate his reputation. He wanted her married, settled, and useful in the way daughters were expected to be.

Atalanta understood the expectations. She simply didn't share them. She wasn't afraid of partnership, but she wasn't willing to give up the life she had built to become a possession in someone else's home. So she did the most honest thing she could: she said no.

The pressure didn't stop. Suitors arrived. Her father insisted. Society had a long list of reasons she should fall in line. Atalanta didn't argue. Instead, she made a choice that reflected her values and protected her freedom. She agreed to marry, but only if a man could outrun her in a fair race. If he couldn't keep up with her, he wasn't meant to be part of her life. A condition like this was unheard of, but Atalanta held her ground. It was her way of saying, "If you want to join me, then meet me where I am."

One after another, suitors challenged her and lost. They all underestimated her, saw her for who they wanted her to be, not for who she was. She left them behind easily, knowing her life was not meant to be shared with a man who did not see her clearly.

Then one day, Atalanta saw Hippomenes and something shifted deep inside her. She liked him. She *really* liked him. And she hoped beyond hope that he would challenge her to a race. She even let herself wonder if he would win.

For his part, Hippomenes knew he couldn't beat Atalanta in a foot race. So he prayed to Aphrodite for help. She gave him three golden apples and told him how to use them.

The day of the race arrived. The two lined up at the start. Even though Atalanta liked Hippomenes, she would not allow him to win. He would have to beat her to win her hand.

The race started and Atalanta took an early lead. Disappointment pricked at her heart, but she would not yield. Then, out of nowhere, a golden apple rolled into her path. Curious and intrigued, she slowed to pick it up and admire it. As she did so, Hippomenes passed her.

Atalanta tucked the apple into her robes and started again, overtaking her challenger easily.

A little while later, another golden apple rolled into her path. She realized it had come from behind her. Again, she picked it up and wondered at it, and again Hippomenes passed her.

She tucked the apple into her robes and once again overtook Hippomenes without breaking a sweat.

Aphrodite could see that her plan was flawed. There was no way Hippomenes could best Atalanta, even with the golden fruit she had given him. So when he rolled his third and final apple past his beloved's feet, Aphrodite charmed it. It grew in size and became unthinkably heavy.

Atalanta bent to pick up the apple and was surprised by its weight. *How can this be?* she thought. Just then, Hippomenes passed her. Atalanta tucked the apple into her robes and chased after Hippomenes, but he crossed the finish line just before her.

And so they got married and lived happily ever after.

Actually, no. Their joy was short-lived, but that's a story for another day.

Finding Your Own True Life

In the traditional telling, Atalanta's myth suggests that any woman, even one as strong and fierce as Atalanta, can be diverted from her goal with the right distraction. But I see it differently.

First of all, Atalanta refused to compromise. Even when she was tempted by the love of a man who pleased her, she maintained her boundary. She didn't enter that race intending to lose. She entered it to learn what sort of man Hippomenes was.

Some say it wasn't a fair race. After all, Hippomenes had a goddess and enchanted golden apples on his side. Wasn't that cheating?

Perhaps. But isn't that how life works? You set a goal. You give it your all. And, from time to time, a golden apple crosses your path. Sometimes it's a shiny bauble you can scoop up and enjoy before continuing on. Sometimes it's big and heavy, and you aren't sure you can bear it. Either way, it's still part of your path.

Maybe the next apple you reach for will lead you to something even better than you thought possible. Maybe it won't. Either way, it's worth finding out.

In the end, Atalanta married, which she had vowed not to do. (Same, girl, same.) But she loved Hippomenes and he loved her. So perhaps that ending was better than the one she had imagined.

For a little while, anyway.

And that's the final piece. The place you land, no matter how wonderful, isn't your last stop. It's just a resting place where you can take stock and think about your next adventure. Because as long as you live, there's always more road to run, and there are always more apples to discover. My story isn't over because I received the love and the farm of my dreams. In a way, it's just beginning.

So take heart. The life you would allow yourself to live will unfold, as it must. And then it will unfold again. That's not a curse to endure. It's literally the reason we're here.

At Undertree Farm

John and I have lived at Undertree Farm for almost three years. We have five horses (including Betty, the blue-eyed paint), ten chickens, two rabbits, and far too many dogs and cats.

We have built a few new buildings and torn some old ones down. We replaced the roof on the house and restored the fireplace. I'm still trying to figure out how grapevines work, but at least the bees have plenty of flowers to visit, and sometimes we even get to harvest some honey.

We have lots of projects planned (baby goats!), but we're in no hurry. For me, that has been the greatest lesson of this place. It doesn't have to be perfect and it doesn't have to be right now. The farm has seasons, and so do we. Meanwhile, the life I'm allowing myself to live is just fine.

Caroline came by a few months ago, and I told her about my dream and how her family inspired me all those years ago. She had no idea, but she thought it was pretty neat.

Me too.

Gentle Calls to Action

Take a moment to sit with your life as it is right now. Notice the tiny choices that are beckoning you. Maybe you feel the tug of curiosity, a quiet longing, or a flicker of desire that won't quite leave you alone. It doesn't even have to be related to your dream. Choose a different restaurant for dinner. Choose a different route for your evening walk. Choose a new ice cream flavor. Just choose differently and see what happens.

Once you get used to making small choices differently, look for the ones that honor the life you want to move toward. Sign up for a class. Volunteer at an animal shelter or rescue. Go to a meetup. Just make sure what you do reflects who you really are inside. This is not a time for performance.

Keep taking small actions that are doable, supportive, and kind. Clear a corner of your day to do something that nourishes you. Not sure what that is? Experiment. Try different things until you figure it out.

Say no to something that drains you, even if everyone's relying on you. Especially if everyone's relying on you. Or say yes to something that gives you butterflies. Remember that fear and excitement are the same emotion, and be brave.

When resistance arises, as it surely will, meet it with the same gentleness you'd offer a dear friend. Change can feel destabilizing, even when it's wanted. You're not supposed to know every step ahead of time. You're not supposed to have the whole map. You're not failing because you feel uncertain. That's the Good Girl talking. You're human. And you're learning how to trust yourself in real time.

As you practice listening to yourself, making new choices, and meeting your fears with kindness, trust that something larger is unfolding beneath the surface. Keep living your truth, and every day you'll become more aligned and more fully your own. Keep choosing yourself and trust the rest will meet you along the way.

Ritual Suggestion

Choose a quiet moment, preferably at the end of the day, when the noise of the world has softened and you can hear your own thoughts. Gather three simple items: a candle, a small dish of salt, and an object that represents possibility to you—a key, a shell, a seed, or anything that feels like a beginning. These will represent clarity, cleansing, and potential.

Place the items in front of you and light the candle. Let the warm glow draw you into your body. Take a few slow breaths, feeling your shoulders drop and your mind loosen its grip. When you're ready, place your hands on your heart and speak aloud: "I allow myself to want more. I allow myself to choose what is mine." Say it three times, letting each repetition sink a little deeper.

Now dip your fingertips into the salt and touch them gently to your palms. This is a symbolic cleansing, an acknowledgment that your hands are capable of shaping a life that honors you. As you brush the salt away, imagine releasing the assumptions, obligations, and expectations that were never truly yours to carry. Let them fall back to the earth where they can dissolve.

Pick up your object of possibility and hold it in your palm. Close your eyes and ask yourself: "What am I ready to invite?" Don't push for an answer. Don't analyze. Just let whatever arises come quietly. When a word, an image, or a feeling emerges, whisper it into the object. Allow it to become a small promise to yourself, a reminder of the life you are willing to live.

When you feel complete, blow out the candle, trusting that the clarity it offered remains with you. Place your chosen object somewhere you'll see it often—a bedside table, a desk, a pocket of your bag. Let it be a touchstone in the days ahead, a gentle nudge back toward the life you are consciously choosing, one step at a time.

Journal Prompts

- When I imagine the life I would allow myself to live, what is the very first feeling that arises in my body?
- What parts of my current life feel aligned with who I'm becoming, and what parts feel like leftovers from an older version of me?
- Where am I still choosing out of fear, habit, or obligation instead of desire or truth?
- What is one small choice I could make this week that would move me closer to the life I want?
- What golden apples have slowed me down in the past, and what did I learn from picking them up?
- Which expectations—mine or others'—am I finally ready to release?
- What would trusting my own timing look like in this season of my life?

- If I stopped trying to earn my worth, how would my days change?
- What do I want more of? What do I want less of?
- Who am I when I stop performing and start listening to myself?

Your Next Step

As you finish this chapter, remember that the life you would allow yourself to live rarely arrives all at once. It comes together in pieces—some chosen and some rolling across your path when you least expect them. You don't have to force clarity or push yourself into dramatic transformation.

Remember all you have learned about yourself during this journey, and keep listening to the quiet truth inside you, the same way Atalanta listened to her instincts as she moved through the forest, the same way you listened when your own life shifted in ways you never could have planned.

There will be seasons of certainty and seasons of doubt. There will be moments when the road ahead is clear and moments when you can barely see a foot in front of you. Trust that both are part of your path, and that every choice—every yes, every no, every pause, every start-again—is shaping something larger than you can see.

Most of all, trust yourself. Trust the woman you've been, the one you're becoming, and the one who is quietly guiding you from within. The life you would allow yourself to live is already reaching for you. All you have to do is keep reaching back, one honest step at a time.

Epilogue

Rising Together

The faint figure behind seemed to shake the pattern, just as if she wanted to get out.

Charlotte Perkins Gilman

In 1887, two years after the birth of her daughter, Charlotte Perkins Gilman was drowning. The heavy weight of depression had pinned her to the ground, and she could not see a way free of it. Today, she would be diagnosed with postpartum depression, a very real and debilitating condition. But in 1887, doctors (virtually all of them men) called it *hysteria*.

Hysteria comes from the Greek word *hystera*, meaning womb. And, in the late 19th century, the treatment was worse than the affliction. It was called "the rest cure."

Women who were subjected to the rest cure were confined to bed. They needed permission to sit up and were not allowed to stand, walk or feed themselves. They were forbidden all intellectual and creative activities. No reading. No writing. No sewing. And no contact with friends or family. The standard treatment lasted for six to eight weeks, but it could go on much longer.

The cause? Doctors explained it was a failure to fulfill their duty to marry and bear children, which caused the uterus to pull up stakes and wander around the body.

Yeah. I don't make the ridiculous medical myths either.

For centuries, the diagnosis of hysteria was a placeholder for everything men did not understand about women. And the cure was to isolate them and starve them of stimulation and connection until they once again submitted to male authority.

When Charlotte Perkins Gilman bravely reached out for help with her depression, she was sent to The Infirmary for Nervous Diseases in Philadelphia, a clinic established by Dr. Silas Weir Mitchell, who developed the rest cure. When her condition did not improve after nine weeks, Mitchell sent her home with these instructions: "Live as domestic a life as possible. Have your child with you all the time. Lie down an hour after each meal. Have but two hours' intellectual life a day. And never touch pen or brush or pencil as long as you live."

Allow me to translate that for you: Be quiet. Be good. Don't make trouble. Don't want too much. Don't step outside the lines.

In 1892, Gilman published a short story called "The Yellow Wallpaper." In it, the faceless, unnamed narrator has been confined to bed by her doctor husband. The walls of her room are covered in a sickly yellow wallpaper. Through the course of the story, as her isolation deepens, the narrator begins to see shapes in that wallpaper, then bars, then women creeping behind the bars, shaking them, desperate to get out.

The women in the yellow wallpaper are all of us.

If 1884 feels like a long time ago, consider that, until the Equal Credit Opportunity Act of 1974, women were not guaranteed the right to open a bank account, apply for a credit card, or get a home loan without their husband's permission. And banks could legally deny unmarried women altogether.

All of this is to say that our generation has an important job to do.

Our daughters are growing up in a world where they can realistically live their lives without the assent of men. And we are the fulcrum, the tipping point between two worlds. We carry a profound responsibility. It's up to us to heal the ancestral trauma our foremothers carried for so long.

> Our grandmothers were the wallpaper survivors.
> Our mothers were the wallpaper rattlers.
> And we are here to tear it all down.

There is so much work left to do, so many women who carry far more than their share—women of color, Indigenous women, LGBTQ+ women (especially trans women), disabled women, women living under oppressive regimes, refugee and undocumented women, and women whose lives are defined by poverty, instability, or danger.

Our awakening is personal. And it is also generational. Ancestral. Collective. It isn't complete until all of us are free.

I hope you will take the words in this book to heart. I hope that you will use them to uncover the truest version of you. The one who has been hiding between the folds of your life.

And then, I hope you will look outward. Tell others what you've discovered. Show them what's possible by living a life that is courageous, fierce, and unapologetically you.

Acknowledgments

This book is the product of lessons learned over many years. If you've been a part of my journey—hero, villain, or somewhere in between—thank you. That includes the person who dedicated a song to Emmerich and me at the sixth grade dance. That wasn't very funny, but I appreciate the material.

To Katherine, who taught me how to love someone more than myself.
To Maureen, who taught me to love old houses.
To Caroline, who taught me to love the country.
To Alison, who always accepted me for who I am.
To John A, who stood by me on all my best and worst days.
To Elaine, who was almost as scared as I was but never showed it.
To J, who trusted me with a very important message.
To Suzanne, whose courage inspired so many great adventures.
To Samson, who amazes me more and more every single day.
To John, every day and twice on Sunday.

And to every furry or feathered friend who has ever loved me: Countess, Winstin, Jasmine, Bella, Captain, Saisho, Leo, Charlotte, Jack, Beau, Buster, Juneaux, Buckingham, Lumpy, Betty, Buddy, Popeye, Calyx, Smoke, Dottie, Hershey, Bianca, and all the chickens. Thank you for keeping me real, laughing, and sane. Mostly.

About the Author

Ann CB Landis is a writer, speaker, and creative guide whose work explores the interior lives of women—the moments we lose ourselves, the courage it takes to return, and the deep magic that rises when we live in alignment with our truth. Her fiction and non-fiction circle the same sacred themes: midlife as initiation, belonging as a birthright, and the quiet power that awakens when women reclaim their lineage of intuition and wisdom.

Born and raised in Maryland, Ann grew up loving horses, words, and the wild spaces that made her feel most like herself. She spent many years building a successful career as a web and software developer before returning to the dream she had as a girl: a small farm where she and her husband, John, could care for horses, grow flowers and herbs, and make things with their hands. That return became both the setting and the spiritual catalyst for *Coming Home to Yourself*.

Today, Ann is surrounded by the things that bring her joy—family, laughter, overgrown gardens, wide-open fields, too many sassy chickens, and the kind of magic that only appears when you allow it. Her days are a blend of writing, caring for animals, and tending the land.

Ann believes it's never to late to remember who you really are. Through her work, she hopes to help other women step into that truth with softness, courage, and a sense of belonging to themselves.

Learn more or drop her a line at annlandis.com.

www.ingramcontent.com/pod-product-compliance
Lightning Source LLC
Chambersburg PA
CBHW071313110426
42743CB00042B/1509